Daydream Journals

First published in 2022
Search Press Limited
Wellwood, North Farm Road,
Tunbridge Wells, Kent TN2 3DR

Reprinted 2022, 2023 (twice)

Photographs by Mark Davison for
Search Press Studios. Styling by Lisa Brown.

ISBN: 978-1-78221-872-2
ebook ISBN: 978-1-78126-841-4

Suppliers
For details of suppliers, please visit the
Search Press website: www.searchpress.com

All the step-by-step photographs in this book
feature the author, Tilly Rose. No models
have been used.

Dedication

I still can't believe I have written a second book!... And yet
I am so happy to be able to share my knowledge and skills
with everyone who reads it. Without the encouragement of
some fabulous women throughout my life, I would never
have arrived at the point where I could share my thoughts.
This book is dedicated to some of the most feisty, beautiful,
strong and yet so very gentle women I have had the
pleasure to meet. I thank each and every one of you for
your beautiful wisdom, strength and encouragement:
Phyllis, my gentle Fen Nan, who was as tough as old boots
and taught me to stay true to my roots, enjoy the ordinary
snippets of life and take one day at a time;
my lovely Aunt Joan, my Fenland inspiration, who taught
me to 'just go for it' – whatever age you may be – and
Rhoda, with whom I have laughed, cried and giggled and
whom I love dearly.
Thank you, ladies
x

Acknowledgements

A few extra words are needed to say a huge thanks
to my lovely editor, May Corfield. Without her
patience and guidance *Daydream Journals* would
not be as sparkling as it is... I thank you dearly,
my lovely friend x

To see more of the author's work, visit:
www.tilly-rose.co.uk
Instagram: @tillyrosevintage
Facebook: Tilly Rose - Textile Artist

Daydream Journals

Memories, ideas & inspiration in stitch, cloth & thread

TILLY ROSE

SEARCH PRESS

Contents

Introduction

Welcome to my
second book and thank you for choosing to
spend some time with me. For anyone who doesn't know
much about me, I am a creative textile artist living in the beautiful
Cambridgeshire Fenlands; an ancient landscape steeped in history, heritage
and wild beauty. I am lucky to be surrounded by Mother Earth's smiles every
single moment of the day and I 'borrow' these for my creations, my workshops
and, of course, for my own daily inspiration, well-being and thoughts.
I love to work and create with cloth and thread, especially pre-loved pieces
that have their own story to tell. And yet I also love to combine them with
other elements such as trimmings, paper, paints, hand stamps, found objects
and treasured mementoes, to help turn them from simple stitched collages into
beautiful symphonies of textures, patterns and gentleness.
I'm guessing if you are reading this that the title of this book may have
intrigued you, or perhaps you simply loved my first book, *Stitched Memories*,
and are interested in finding out a little more. I wrote a section in my first book
about my daydream journals, hoping that I could expand it a little with more
detail in a second book… and here I am!
I have always loved writing and doodling. The idea of keeping some form of
diary sketchbook to combine the two in order to preserve precious memories,
creative stories, thoughts and inspirations that help me with my stitched work,
really appealed. But I found the actual part of making such a sketchbook
really hard. Every New Year, I would diligently try to start a new diary with the
good intention of being organized, but by February my daily entries would be
dwindling and, after a busy day at work, I would forget what I wanted to add to
it. I seemed to be forever failing and – I hold my hands up – I got bored easily.
I would daydream and waste time. And yet I loved writing so much. And even
more, I loved doodling in a little book, which meant so much to me.
I eventually gave up trying to conform to the norm
(like most things) and decided to venture
on my own path.

Back then, it wasn't really called journalling. I found that if I just jotted down snippets of ordinary life in doodle form, notes, lists, or just as a simple ideas page, then I would refer to it again and again when designing a new project.

I discovered that if I called it my 'Daydream Journal' it didn't really matter what I put in it. I could flit all over the place, wherever and whenever it suited me, and it didn't matter that there was no order. It also didn't matter that it wasn't making sense as such to anyone else, and it certainly didn't matter if I went wrong. For me, I had found my happy place.

By now you may be thinking: but what is a daydream journal? And, more importantly, who is this book aimed at? I can answer that by simply saying that it is aimed at anyone who has a creative mind, who loves to find inspiration in the ordinary snippets of life, who loves to dabble with cloth and thread, or maybe enjoys a little mixed-media textile art – and will hopefully enjoy discovering a new path of exploration once they have allowed themselves to delve into the lovely land of curiosity comprising 'what ifs'.

We all daydream throughout the day, wherever we may be, and those with a creative mind will appreciate the fun my style of daydream journalling can bring. Sometimes trying to hold on to those creative thoughts long enough to add to a project can cause worry.

'Daydreams… a beautiful place where you can lose time, forget your everyday thoughts, sing all day and encourage a gentle curiosity.'

You may not consider yourself to be a journaller because you don't keep a diary, or you may think you can't keep a sketchbook because you are unable to draw. Over the following pages, I am hoping to persuade you to think differently. I want to introduce you to my world of inspirations, a way of capturing the ordinary snippets of life, and to help you feel brave enough to discover new ideas and maybe even give it a go.

I will explain why I use a journal and how it helps with designing my stitched projects; I will offer you a host of techniques to help you create your own journals which will, in turn, help you to create some beautiful slow-stitched projects.

Finally, a note to say that the step-by-step instructions in the projects section show 'demonstration' pieces to explain how to make them, rather than the actual pieces in the styled photography; this is because of the time it takes to make some of the projects and the unique cloth that I used in many of them.

I hope you have fun and enjoy trying out my ideas for yourself!

Tilly x

Inspiration

WHERE TO BEGIN

As a textile artist and tutor, the main question I am always asked is: 'Where do you get your inspiration from?' I would need a whole book just to answer that query! 'Inspiration' is a big word that can encompass a lifetime of experiences, or simply capture a fleeting moment during your day. It is a deeply personal thing and what works for one person won't work for another.

Someone who loves the colour green will meet several others in their lifetime who cannot abide it. We are all individual and therefore our inspirations will be, too.

In this section, I cover what makes me smile as a way of getting started. I explain where I find inspiration and how it helps with my crafting projects.

Throughout the book, I talk about the following items in a little more detail, but for now I think the easiest way of telling you where I find my inspiration is simply to make a list (see right).

* Mother Earth – capturing each season through colours, textures, patterns and smells
* Pressed flowers, leaves, seedpods
* Vintage patterns, designs and ephemera
* Descriptions of scenes, poems, old books
* Old photographs, old postcards
* Fashion and accessories from different eras
* Social stories
* Patterns on old cloth, lace or trims
* Museums, galleries and old buildings
* Architecture and social history
* Books, literature and plays
* Folklore, song lyrics and old tales

You can probably guess that I have absolutely loads of journalling notebooks that I have collected over the years, and each one tells its own story, full of thoughts and inspirations. Inside you will find snippets of all kinds of things that bring a little smile, however silly they may seem to others. I love nothing more than grabbing a cup of tea, finding my favourite spot and sifting through my notebooks on a rainy day to reminisce.

They are my memories captured in words, doodles, thoughts, pieces of cloth and snippets of everyday found objects that I have used for designs, stitched projects or simply want to use again and again.

They are diaries, reference books, notes, lists of often unfinished plans, scribbled recipes, dates of days out, collections of photographs, doodles for designs and scripted pieces planned for all kinds of possibilities. And they all make me smile.

I'm a big believer in serendipity and often a journal capturing one thing at the beginning invariably finishes on a completely different path (a little like my thought processes most of the time!). The secret is not to overthink things and not to try to complete a book with too many rules. Try to let your creativity flow.

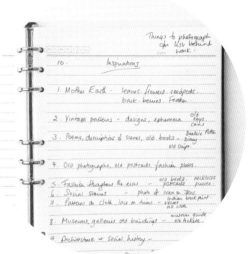

As I am always saying: there are no rules. It is a daydream journal, not a reference book being published for a library. Allow yourself to have some fun with it. Allow it to simply be the idea of creating a beautiful safe place to visit when you have a moment.

The beauty of daydream journals is that, one day, they will become family heirlooms in their own right. Remember that stories never finish – they simply turn into the beginnings of a new adventure.

– Explore – Play – Create – Be Free – Doodle – Sketch – Write – Fun –

FINDING EVERYDAY INSPIRATIONS

'The true secret of happiness lies in taking a genuine interest in all the details of daily life.'

William Morris

Finding out what inspires you may sound easy, but I know for some it can seem very daunting. Having taught for many years in a variety of situations and environments, I would also say that inspirations won't come knocking on your door. You have to open your eyes and really look for things. You have to wait for the magic to happen. And when I say look, I mean *really* look.

Here's a little exercise to get started:

1 Stand still or sit still, right where you are as you are reading this.
2 Close your eyes if you prefer but if you do, read the next few steps first!
3 Now take a slow breath in and forget the world for a few minutes.
4 What can you hear?
5 What can you smell?
6 Now open your eyes and look at something close to you that catches your eye. Look at the shape, the pattern and the design.

7 How would you describe it in three words?
8 Keep it simple – remember, don't overthink it. This is not a test to set you up to fail. It is simply a reminder to take a few minutes to appreciate the simplicity of using your senses for no other reason than three little words.

Now ask yourself, how often have you actually taken the time to really look at that object? I bet most of you would say it's been there for years and I've only just really noticed it. In reality, we do this with our surroundings and thoughts all the time, which is why so many of us may miss the obvious inspiration standing right in front of us.

It may be that little patch of flowers you pass every morning as you walk the dog. You know they are there, and they look pretty, but have you ever bent down, smelt the blossom and looked at the shape of their leaves? It may be a painting hanging on the wall of your favourite coffee shop – remember to look at the figures in the painting, and their shapes and colours. Or it could be a favourite scarf your mum wears all the time and yet you don't notice it.

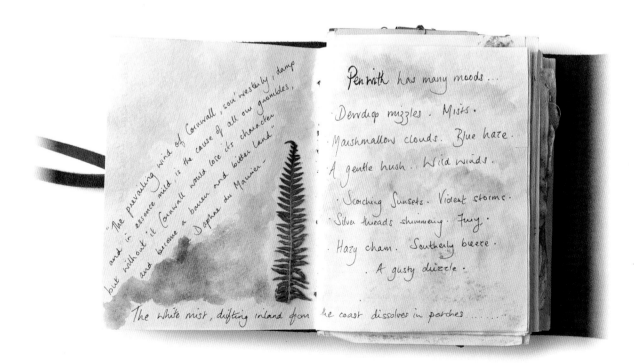

Once you've opened your mind to embracing all the things around you, it will be quite addictive. I have had people tell me that they never stop looking once they have realized what has actually been right in front of their eyes all the time! They now notice the tiny detail of a season, the words in a favourite song, or even the colour of their favourite flower.

Don't forget to include your family in your inspirations; remember conversations, little family sayings, quotes using local dialect, and so on. Look at their clothes, and note down the little things they say or even sing. They are all beautiful inspirations that surround us each and every day and will mean something personal to you.

Write these things down in your journal as keepsakes and memories, and you can always use them in stitched projects if you have them to refer back to.

Draw pictures or doodles of particular signs, words or get your children or grandchildren to draw in your book for you.

How wonderful would it be to stitch a flower your grandson drew after a walk home from school together? Tell his story for him in your stitched threads.

One last thing I need to mention here is photographs. Most people have mobile phones these days, so capturing a moment or phrase with a photograph can be invaluable if you haven't anything else to hand to record your observations.

KEEPING A DAYDREAM JOURNAL

'You don't write because you want to say something, you write because you have something to say.'

F. Scott Fitzgerald

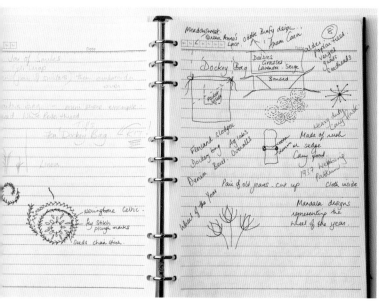

I'm often asked why I bother to keep a journal when I explain to my classes and workshop students what it is that I do. 'So, what is the point?', people ask, and 'What do I do with it?' There are many answers to those questions.

Keeping an inspirational journal, in whatever form, is a very personal choice. It can be a diary, a sketchbook, a scribble pad or simply a doodle pad. Often at the start of a new year, many of the above are purchased by people with the intention of making notes for a new craft, keeping a diary throughout the year, or for drawing new designs.

But, in reality, what that actually means is for the first few weeks it will be used with real intent, and then gradually the joy of keeping up the momentum turns into nothing but a pain and becomes a chore. The journal is either stashed away in a drawer for the rest of the year, or left to gather dust on the shelf, through fear of becoming too much like hard work. Sound familiar?

So my aim is to try to persuade you otherwise. I'm hoping that with a few simple pointers, a gentle guiding hand and a little encouragement, you'll feel able to explore the joy of keeping your own daydream journal and using it in a way that will help with your craft projects as you refer back to it for your own inspiration.

It will also be a way of allowing yourself some time to indulge in creative thoughts; a way of looking after your own well-being. So let's start at the very beginning.

One of the most important elements of keeping a journal of any kind is allowing yourself a few minutes during the day to sit and gather your thoughts. This can be first thing in the morning over breakfast, last thing at night before you retire to bed, or it could be during your tea break while working a busy shift.

The important thing to remember is that no matter what, for those few minutes, it will be entirely your time. I often take my journal with me on walks, day trips, holidays and always when I'm stopping off for coffee. We often forget that our immediate environment can be just as inspiring as a grand stately home and garden may be, and can inspire us in ways we may never even have thought of before.

I captured these foxgloves while out walking early one morning when on holiday in Cornwall, simply using watercolour pens. I just adored the richness of their colour as they bobbed about in the Cornish breeze – a beautiful way of capturing a little memory.

Taking the first steps

The first question to consider when starting to create your daydream journal is: What are you going to do with it once you begin writing or doodling?

You really don't need a final objective in order to start one. You just need to decide that you would like to venture into a new project and see where it leads you. For me, I love nothing more than whiling away a few moments over a cup of tea, doodling without rhyme or reason.

'But what if I can't draw?', I hear you ask. The simple answer is that you don't need to be able to draw. You don't need an art degree, or even a special set of art pens. You just need a pen or pencil you feel comfortable using, and a notebook or notepad to write in. It doesn't have to be an expensive notebook filled with artist-quality cartridge paper, or a watercolour sketchpad – the cheapest option from a supermarket will do.

Be guided by the paper. Are the pages a particular paper you like? How thick is the paper? Is it suitable to pop in your handbag for work? These are all questions only you can answer. It will be your journal, so if you choose to work with cerise pink pages, go with it. It has to be something that makes you smile!

Personally, I prefer to use an A5 hardback book (148 x 210cm/5¾ x 8¼in) to start off. It offers me a stable base I can work on wherever I use it, at home on the sofa, in a café over a cup of coffee, or on a sandy beach on a summer's day. I can rest it on my lap comfortably and pack it away in a small bag if need be, making it easily transportable and a constant companion.

I prefer my pages to be plain paper of watercolour quality so that I can paint or colour wash the pages to my own design. However, you may prefer plain lined pages as a guide to get started, especially if you are planning on more of a diary-style journal. Alternatively, you could also use an old hardbook from a charity/thrift shop if you wish and either stick in your own styled pages over the originals, or colour wash the pages and use them as your base.

So, once you've chosen your notebook, what's the next step? As in all my projects, tips and suggestions, the next important step is to make it your own. It has to feel like a friend who you can talk to each day. You have to feel comfortable with it as your companion, and feel you want to take it everywhere you go. For me, that comes naturally, as I have been journalling for so many years now, but if it is new to you, be gentle on yourself. Like any new friendship, it will take time to evolve, and this will develop at its own pace – don't overthink it. This is not a project that can be rushed and may never be finished. It has no rules and you have no fixed agenda. Like any beautiful flower, it will need a wonderful mixture of sunny days and showery raindrops!

WRITTEN WORDS

... dew underfoot ...

Adopt the pace of Nature; Her secret is patience

Forsythia sunt...

I have always had a love for language, especially old forgotten words, local dialect or even words borrowed from faraway lands. Words have a rich history all of their own. They hold secrets from our past, tell stories and capture treasured memories. Even if you don't know the meaning of a word, you can fall in love with it for no other reason than that it sounds romantically gentle, quirky or funny.

Words nestled together like a string of pearls can help transform an ordinary moment into something very special. We learn language from the day we are born; and, like cloth, it surrounds us for the whole of our lives in one way or another. From a young age we learn to use language to describe our feelings, emotions, thoughts, our happiness and even our sadness. Jumbles of letters form words, just as stitches joined together on cloth form patterns and designs. Through language and a love of cloth and thread, we are able to tell stories using the inspiration of everyday things that surround us.

So, where am I going with this? Capture everything you see, everything you hear and everything you feel in words. Write single words or try sentences. Jot them down in your journal in random places. They don't have to make sense. You are simply using your journal as a reference tool, like an old-fashioned encyclopedia that only you will see. When you feel a little more confident you can write down your daydreams, too. But where do you find words? Here are some ideas:

> * poems * stories * tales * letters * postcards * old diaries * bills * quotes * flyers * tickets * marketing blurbs * magazines * online searches * posters * café conversations * films * radio * song lyrics * restaurant gossip * shops * holidays * buses * trains * craft group *

Sun bleached parched patchwork ...

Billowy downsy seedhead ...

The list goes on, and this is where you can allow your thoughts to wander and meander. From one simple word, a beautiful creative project could evolve.

Here's a little exercise to try over a cuppa:

1 Grab a pen and paper.
2 Set a timer for five minutes.
3 Write down as many things that pop into your mind as you can – for example, cherry blossom. (Did you think of candy-floss colours, or perhaps springtime?)

It's a brilliant way of making you stop and think. Why not try it with your sewing group perhaps? It will not only encourage conversation among you all, but will also help a few ideas to blossom.

shimmers in the scorching mid-summer

DOODLES

Doodles are not masterpieces. They are simply drawn meandering lines that wander all over your paper or cloth, creating a beautiful symphony of shapes that, when joined together, make a wonderful mosaic.

The secret to success is not to worry if your doodles are not perfectly symmetrical, realistic or factually correct. Doodles should be free-flowing like dancing ice skates on a Fenland winter's day. They don't have to make sense. Little squiggly lines, curvy waves and a few dots here and there can produce a wonderful waltz. This can then be used as a border in a stitch design, or perhaps an edging design in a notebook.

A few things to consider below will follow. Your answers may just spark a handful of ideas to help you along the way:

+ Do you want any written words such as poems, or a few daily thoughts?
+ Consider capturing precious moments in time, such as family weddings, bereavements, holidays and celebrations.
+ Think about making a university going-away journal, including encouraging words from the family.
+ Make early morning lists over a cuppa.
+ Keep travel mementoes – list of journeys, keepsakes.
+ What are your favourite colours?
+ Seasons; what are your favourite inspirations?
+ Which wildflower names do you like?
+ Decide what type of pen you prefer to write with.

TOOLS AND MATERIALS

Whenever you start a new project there is often a worry that you will need lots of new equipment, but I want to reassure you that really you don't need to go and buy lots of stuff. You just need to find what works for you. I've listed some of my favourites for creating a journal as a guide.

Pens

It is important to find out what you prefer to write or doodle with, so just have fun exploring. Perhaps you could borrow a friend's pens before purchasing if that helps, simply because what works for one person may not suit another, and you don't want to purchase items you won't subsequently use. Crafting buddies are always generous, so you're bound to be offered a variety to choose from.

Biros   Cheap and cheerful, easily accessible from most supermarkets and stationers. Watch out for 'blots' and 'bleeds'.

Traditional ink pens   I love using these. They can produce some beautiful effects, but can also be very messy. They can bleed on the page and stain your fingers when you refill them, but persevere, as they feel wonderful when they glide over the paper with the fluidity of a pair of ice-skates on the ice. As a result, you will produce some absolutely gorgeous designs with a retro feel.

Rollerball pen   This is a modern-day version of an old-fashioned ink pen without the fuss of any messy ink. These are good for encouraging a curvy style of handwriting over the page rather than getting 'stuck' in the thickness of your paper as can happen when using a biro.

Micron pens   These are often a favourite with many designers and doodlers alike, and come in a variety of thicknesses, allowing smaller details to be easily added. Waterproof and fade-proof, they are an essential tool in your creative pencil case, as you can use them on cloth too.

Pencils

A soft HB pencil is a lovely choice if you want to add a delicate, vintage, faded extra something to a design created with a pen. It is also good for drawing designs if you are worried about making mistakes, as you can simply rub out the hiccups and carry on working. Pencils are also very convenient to take with you for sketching when you are out and about.

Coloured pencils

You really can't go wrong with a cheap set of pencil crayons – the sort you can find while doing your weekly shop or in your local post office. Be guided by the colours. Once you start to settle into journalling, you may wish to invest in a more expensive set, but it is really not essential. Use them to add a subtle shade of colour to a background, or a little gentle detail here and there. They come in a wonderful range of colours from soft pastels to brighter, more vibrant colours.

Watercolour pens

These can be found in any artist's or stationery shop and can be used as a felt-tip style pen or, when added to water, offer a rainbow of ombre shades that will transform your work. Follow the advice of each individual maker as to how to store and use them.

Watercolour pencils

These are simply water-soluble coloured pencils that you dip in water to use, and they are really useful. You can also use them dry. As the colour is encased in a pencil, you can sharpen it if you want a really fine line.

Watercolour paints

A small paintbox is perfect as it is easily transportable if you are taking it with you on walks. You may want a few options to mix your colours on, such as plastic lids or saucers.

Paintbrushes

I like to keep a selection of sizes and thicknesses to play around with. A mixed set will help to get you started.

Useful extras

A few other extra items I keep in readiness are:

- ✦ Glue stick
- ✦ Sticky tape
- ✦ Ink pads
- ✦ Hand stamps
- ✦ Paper clips
- ✦ Pins
- ✦ Safety pins
- ✦ Natural jute string
- ✦ Scissors (for paper)
- ✦ Sketchbooks
- ✦ Watercolour journal

I don't always have a journal with me, despite trying my best to remember, so I often use the paper I find on my travels. Old envelopes make good instant notelets, café serviettes create the perfect instant back up, and I always keep all my unwanted printouts to use as recycled paper. Always remember to reuse wherever possible to help protect our planet.

A useful suggestion, when you have a few spare minutes, is to wander around the house and see what oddments you can find to keep in a stash box in readiness for when you need a quick go-to project.

COLLECTING SNIPPETS

Your journal should be a lovely raggle-taggle of ideas, treasured snippets and found objects that you use as your inspiration. Therefore, one of the most enjoyable parts of the process is collecting all your lovely goodies together as you find them.

I collect anything and everything I find on my travels. Nothing is missed, and I do mean nothing! Sometimes they are used for creating my journal, others are simply keepsakes. Below is a list of all kinds of items that may inspire you to experiment in your journal.

Paper

This can be torn, cut, coloured, ripped, stamped and painted on, or simply added as a keepsake. I use things such as newspapers, magazine cuttings, old documents, rescued pages from old books, old envelopes, tickets, sheet music and postcards.

Photographs

You can use pictures from your walks, holidays, day trips or any others that have meaning for you.

Haberdashery items

I love using items such as ribbons, lace, odd buttons, tags, curtain tape and elastic.

Found objects

Keys, coins, tickets, cotton reels, spoons, buttons and labels are all useful items to use.

Natural treasures

These can be things collected from nature walks such as feathers, twigs, stones, leaves, flowers, pebbles, shells and moss.

So we have all the essentials to get started, but how do we find the time? This is something that should not be an extra on your daily tick list – it should be a part of your normal everyday creative thought process. When you overhear a funny snippet of conversation on the bus going to work; or you spot a quirky quote on a wall in your local café, or even hear something funny on the radio… all of these can be used as inspiration or as a prompt for a memory. You may never use them, or they could make the perfect match for adding to the next cross-stitch design you are creating for a loved one's special birthday.

23

Techniques

Over the next few pages I have given you a few of my favourite tips and techniques to make your journal sing. It is difficult to separate some of the techniques into just paper or cloth, as there is so much overlap, and I combine them all the time. I suggest you simply have fun dabbling and experimenting with all kinds of options and find out what suits you best.

CREATING PAGES AND BACKGROUNDS

I like to personalize plain white and cream pages with my own subtle tones of colour, as it helps me feel calmer when doodling. You may prefer a brighter shade yourself, but do remember that the brighter the colour, the stronger your doodles, quotes and words need to be in order to stand out.

Adding any kind of colour to a design can be quite scary in so many ways, but starting with a blank white page can be even scarier. Colour can be quite tricky to get right. Too much can be a bold statement and too little can be wishy-washy, so let's start gently. Listed below are a few of my favourite options. Once you have dabbled and feel a little more confident, then you can increase the intensity of your colours.

Colour washes

Start by choosing a couple of your favourite watercolours to experiment with. On a dry page and using a fairly thick paintbrush, gently brush over a thin layer of cold water. Allow it to seep slowly into the page. Before it dries, you can then gently add a dash of watercolour paint from your paintbox. Your paper may curl a little, so make sure you place your pages on a waterproof base to protect your work surface.

I like to use an old-fashioned bone-china saucer for my mixing palette, but you can use anything you have to hand, such as an artist's moulded palette, a clean yoghurt pot or an old teacup. If you are working outside, then you could use an old plastic lid or something similar that's easy to carry around in your bag.

As well as using a paintbox, you can use watercolour pens to create a colour wash (see opposite).

1 When I am using a watercolour pen, I start scribbling a few lines with the pens onto my china plate and mix in a little water to create my own paint as a starting base.

2 I then dip my wet paintbrush gently into the colour and add a wash to the page by allowing the brush to flow in any direction.

It is important to experiment to find out your preferred way of working. I keep adding colour slowly until I'm happy with the depth of the shade. As your colour dries, you will get a beautiful ombre effect of shades, especially if you allow the colour to 'pool' a little on the page with an extra drop of water. Don't forget to allow each page to dry before moving on to the next one, to prevent your pages sticking together.

Try experimenting with the following:

+ Felt-tip pens
+ Inks
+ Natural dyes
+ Petal wash (see page 39)
+ Squishing a still-warm herbal teabag across the page.

I often use a dry watercolour pen to finish off the page edge.

The finished colour wash; once dry, the page is ready to use.

Creating a vintage style

As you might guess, I don't like a polished, brand-new look to my journals. I prefer them to have a beautiful old-fashioned vintage effect comprising ripped pages, ragged edges and dulled colours to combine with all the bright pops of colour I add while using them. The two together create a beautiful marriage. You may enjoy some of the techniques here if you wish to add an extra flavour of nostalgia to your journal.

A vintage nostalgia

You can dull your pages from bright white to a vintage 'antiquey' look by covering your pages with a diluted wash of coffee or tea. Leave a little of your usual cuppa to go cold and then add a few more drops of cold water to dilute it a little further. Paint it directly onto your pages in the same way as a colour wash, except your pages are dry to start this time. Allow each page to dry before starting the next one.

Ripped edges

Simply rip a few pages along the outer edge to add an aged look by pulling the paper from the top in a downward motion (see below). Do this slowly so you have a little control. You can choose to do all your pages or just the odd page here and there. I like the novelty of a few here and there. You can add a further vintage feel to them by dabbing the edges with a used teabag to accentuate the ripped edges (see below right).

Rubber stamping

You may be surprised that I have included this in a book connected to stitching, but I love adding stamped extras to all of my work, and especially my inspirational journals. It connects paper to cloth, textile art to design and helps to personalize a project.

I'm not a paper crafter or a card maker, so stamps for me simply add a flavour of design or texture. I'm not worried if the stamp prints are not a perfect image, as this only adds a vintage feeling to my work, especially when using them on cloth.

The burning question is always which stamp pad to use with the stamps. I'm guided completely by colour and colour alone. My stamped pieces are never washed, so I am not worried about using permanent inks, but this is something you need to bear in mind if you are adding stamps to something that will eventually be laundered.

The process for me is exactly the same whether on cloth or paper. The only thing you need to decide is what kind of stamp design takes your fancy.

You will need:

A piece of cloth (I used calico)
A rubber stamp (I used a design from my own Summer Sparkle collection)
An ink pad
A foam mat
Baby wipes
An acrylic block

1 First place your chosen stamp onto an acrylic block for ease of use. These come in a variety of sizes to accommodate different designs and will need space around your stamp to hold it comfortably. Place your cloth over a foam mat for better accuracy before stamping. This will also help prevent any seepage of excess ink onto your work surface.

3 Turn over the inked stamp by holding the acrylic block and place it directly onto the cloth. It is important not to move it at this stage to avoid producing a blurred image. Press down firmly but gently. This will allow the ink to transfer from the rubber stamp to your cloth.

2 Gently dab the ink pad onto the stamp to load it with colour. Don't be heavy handed and over-ink it, as you will get a 'sludgy' look.

Tips

If you press too firmly you will get an uneven design, so practise first to help build your confidence.

Allow your design to dry before adding it to another project.

4 Repeat as many times as you want the design to appear.

You can repeat this process on different pieces of cloth, as well as different kinds of paper. Experiment with building up your designs with different colours, motifs and patterns. Other textures to try include paper, such as handmade, cartridge, printer, wrapping paper, old books, sheet music, newspapers, magazines; card, such as old birthday cards, cardboard, recycled packaging; and cloth, such as cottons, linens, silk, satin, voile and netting.

After stamping you will need to clean off any build-up of ink residue left on the stamp. I use a baby wipe for this or a wet cotton cloth and simply dab off any residual ink. You can alternatively use a rubber stamp cleaner.

Indian block printing

I love to use all kinds of options when printing pieces of cloth to add to collages or journals, but block printing is one of my absolute favourites. I feel a wonderful connection with tradition and nature when using the wooden blocks, knowing they have their own story to tell through their grain and tactile touch. They help ground my thoughts while printing, and I love the connection to days gone by with such an ancient skill.

The traditional art of block printing originates from India and is continued today by artisans using skills passed down throughout the generations from father to son. Primarily, block prints were used for cloth design, but they are very versatile and lend themselves to all kinds of media if you are brave enough to experiment.

The following steps show how I used a block that I designed while in Jaipur, on both cloth and paper, but you may like to experiment with other ideas. You will get so many different results once you start.

1 Spread some acrylic paint onto a saucer. I find a teaspoon is good for this, but you can purchase specific spreaders designed for the job if you prefer. Dab a sponge into the paint gently to build up a layer.

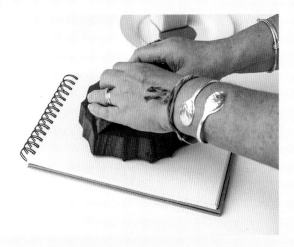

2 Dab your sponge onto the block. Make sure you do this gently in stages, repeating step 1 several times to get an even coating, otherwise you will get a 'claggy' look.

3 Turn the block over and place it gently onto your surface. I printed directly into my journal, but if you prefer to use it on cloth, place a tea towel underneath your work to cushion it, which will allow the block to make good contact with the threads of the cloth and help to produce a firmer print. Press firmly but don't move the block.

Below I printed directly onto a piece of calico, which I will then stitch over. It could then be added to a slow-stitched collage.

4 Gently lift off the block, using the edges, to reveal your finished design. Allow the paint to dry before using it in a project.

A gallery of ideas

Below are some examples of how I have experimented with different rubber-stamp designs and Indian blocks using a variety of colours and different textures.

In the example above, I used my own rubber stamps to create a repeating pattern. I then transferred this idea onto a piece of calico to create a collage of slow stitching.

My bunny design evolved from some ideas I had while playing with some Indian blocks on paper. You can see how, after creating the background using different colours with my blocks, I then added lots of stitching to create a piece of textile art that will eventually be framed.

The bunny stamp in detail.

Scrapbook style

Scrapbook journalling combines typical diary or journal writing with the craftiness of scrapbooking. It is often associated with a certain styled craft with particular rules such as adding written details in a structured way, or by way of placement of mementoes and so on. I borrow some of these techniques to add to my daydream journals, but in a very gentle manner.

I have no particular order for placing collected things on pages, or the way I write. I don't like perfect or accurate details as it doesn't reflect who I am as an artist, but you may prefer a little more order to your journal, so go with what works for you.

To add even more depth to my journals I like to add tabs, markers and pockets that help create a family within my journals, holding secrets, messages, memories, reminders and so on.

The photograph above shows how my thoughts and ideas, taken from a walk at Woodwalton Fen, inspired me to design a border that I later added to an exhibition quilt. It was based on the flora and fauna of the Fens. I dried a piece of fern to remind me of the autumn colours and to match my drawing. My design evolved from a few quick doodles to the end result of the drawn border you can see at the extreme right of the photograph. I later stitched this design using free motion embroidery.

The example below shows how I was experimenting with ideas for creating my own winter greetings cards with some quick doodles.

Pockets, tabs and borders

To add depth to my journals I like to add tabs, markers and pockets that help create a family within my journals, holding secrets, messages, memories, reminders and so on. I stamp or write on paper and cloth, add old envelopes for pockets and sometimes even create cloth patches.

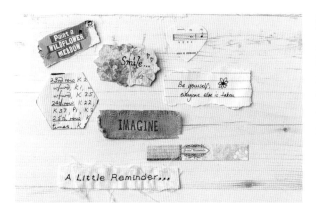

Here I've experimented with ideas to create a collection of words using a mixture of handwritten snippets, stamped designs on cloth, torn magazine pieces and sheet music.

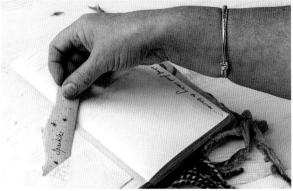

I love adding words or doodles into journal pockets as a little something extra from me that remains a secret between me and the future reader. I imagine my reader several generations from now finding lovely surprises from me to cheer their day! You may like to include dates, quotes, memories, or, as I've suggested, little messages for future generations to find.

Borders can be such fun to add to your journals and make them individual. You can create them with simple doodles, stamps, drawn lines or even ribbons or lace. I created a few border templates for you to use on pages 126–127. Why not try creating little families of words and collected items? Group together colours, topics, shapes and so on. It can be quite addictive once you start.

Creating a journal wrap template

Journal covers or wraps make each notebook personal. If you are using a shop-bought notebook, you may wish to cover it with a design that reflects its contents. You will find a few examples of how to create a stitched wrap cover in the projects on pages 64, 70 and 78.

To create a foundation base for your wrap you will need a piece of calico or cotton bigger than your notebook by at least 5cm (2in) all the way around.

1 Cut out a piece of calico or cotton – it can be an old pillowcase, tablecloth or man's shirt – and place the journal or notebook on it.

2 Fold in the edges of each side to create the flaps.

3 Close the book with the flaps enclosed. This will allow an 'ease' around your book.

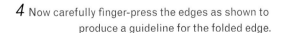

4 Now carefully finger-press the edges as shown to produce a guideline for the folded edge.

5 Open the book again so that the pressed edges are visible.

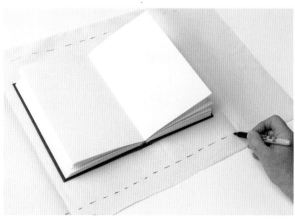

6 Draw a dashed line all the way across the calico template with a felt-tip pen roughly 5cm (2in) above the book, and then repeat on the lower edge.

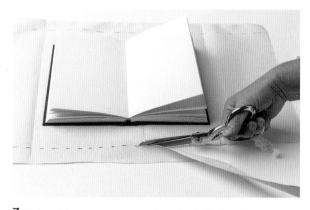

7 Using fabric scissors, cut along both dashed lines.

8 Fold the lower edge of the calico up by about 2.5cm (1in) and finger press to produce a fold line.

9 Turn the book around and repeat for the top edge.

10 You will now be able to comfortably wrap the book template around the book on the left-hand side with the flap tucked under.

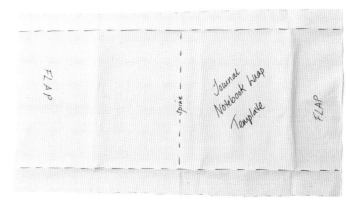

11 Repeat step 10 for the right-hand side.

12 Remove the calico and label the flaps and spine as above, marking all the dashed lines along the fold marks, so that you can use it as a template for future journal projects. I have not added seam allowances or any other measurements on mine, but you can write on your calico template to suit your own projects as a reminder, if you wish.

Working with Mother Earth

Feeling connected with Mother Earth is in my DNA; my Fen roots. It's an important factor that flows through all my designs. My family history originates from a very long line of agricultural labourers (known as 'ag labs') who toiled the Fenland for many hours every day, and often in very harsh conditions.

They learnt to recognize the importance of knowing their seasons, their local flora and fauna and understanding the importance of how having a mutual respect for nature worked in their favour.

I love to use natural dyes and colour palettes in my designs when I can, and that also includes my journals or diaries. I also love to experiment with all kinds of options. While out walking, if I find a little treasure such as a wildflower, a misshapen twig or simply a battered autumn leaf that has survived a Fenland storm, I like to pop them into my pocket for a little reminder of my walk. A patch of 'weeds' on a roadside verge or a little group of dandelions hiding among the grass on a verge somewhere can also be the perfect paint palette for a colour wash on a page of my journal or on a cloth background for a stitched project.

I love to use wildflowers for inspiration. Take a moment to recognize their colour, their composition, their scent and get to know them a little better. How many petals do they have? What shape are they? Where do they grow? How do you preserve those colours? Listed on the following pages are just a few of my favourite techniques that you may like to experiment with.

Always remember to wash your hands after touching flowers and plants, as some can cause skin rashes or other sensitivities.

Flower squishing

This is as simple as it sounds. Simply pick up the flowers in your fingers and squish them onto the paper. You can try rubbing in a circular motion, depending on the shape of the petals. You will have varied results with this technique, depending on what time of day you find your flowers and what season you are in.

Before noon is the best option for freshly picked petals. Do remember to pick only a modest amount – just what you need – and always make sure there are lots of flowers left behind for the insects, and to go to seed so that they can make more plants for the following year.

This shows the effects of squishing rose petals on the right and evening primrose on the left (above).

Once I've completed squishing the flowers I want to use, I make notes about them, including which flowers I used (see above). I recommend doing this, otherwise it's easy to forget what you've done! It is also useful to have a record of which flower produces which colour, for future reference. There are often surprises; for example, the buddleia I used here produced a browny-yellow colour, even though the petals are lilac.

Flower tapping

If you are doing this on a single piece of paper, you will need to place a soft towel or flannel underneath the paper to protect your work surface. If, like me, you are using a drawing pad, just be aware that the colour from the flower you are tapping may bleed through to the next page. Remember that you are capturing their beauty, not smashing them to pieces, so be gentle and respectful. This process can be a little like very fast flower pressing in that sometimes the petals adhere to the page. I like to leave them there, but you can peel them off if you prefer.

Try different flowers at different times of the year. Each will give you a different effect and colour.

1 Place the flowers face down on the paper, making sure all the petals are as flat as possible. This may be tricky with large blooms, so you may need to adjust them until you are happy with their position. Lay a piece of kitchen paper on top and, using a 'weight', you can tap them down. I used an antique wooden bobbin I've treasured for years, as it has a flat bottom and is perfect for not damaging the flowers. You could use a small can of beans, a pottery mug or even a small sewing ham.

2 Once you have tapped your flowers three or four times, pull back the kitchen paper very gently to reveal the colour that has transferred to the notepad. Sometimes the petals will stick to the paper like the cranesbills have (see above). I'm happy to leave some to dry on the page as it is a reminder of my walk and will help me remember which flower I used.

I like to experiment with a wide variety of different flowers (see right). Here I have used buttercups, cranesbills, fuchsias and hydrangea petals.

You could also try some of these flowers: buddleia, roses, cornflowers, wallflowers, primroses, daffodils, crocuses, pelargoniums, poppies and golden rod.

You can use this method for capturing flowers on cloth and then stitch over them. However, please remember that the colours are not colourfast, so choose your petals wisely.

Petal wash

Flower petals provide a gorgeous palette of colours that can be used to make a petal wash, which you can apply with a paintbrush. I find these useful for giving just a hint of colour to a sheet of white paper, which can be your starting point for a journal page before you begin to embellish it and add all the other elements you intend to include. Alternatively, you can use it to add colour to fabrics that you are working on.

1 Simply drop a handful of petals into a mug of freshly boiled water and allow them to steep for at least ten minutes as if you were making herbal tea. Allow to cool.

2 The petals will release their swirling mists of colour and you can use this as a colour wash. If you're working on paper, as I am here, note that the richness of the colours will be affected by the type of paper you use.

Try experimenting with different types of petals to see what colours you get. For my page above I used marigolds and rose campion, both of which release their colour quite readily. The dry page is shown left.

Berry squishing

Berries provide a riot of colour in a variety of ways. Squishing them onto paper is a little messy but very addictive, as you can create patterns, textures and a wonderful blend of colour tones. (You can also use them to create your own 'watercolours' using the method on page 39.) Make sure the berries are at room temperature when you use them, as they release their juices better than when they are cold.

You will find that some berries produce deeper colours than others, so just experiment to find what you want for your particular project. Once the berry juice has dried, the colour will fade slightly.

1 Here I am using a blueberry. You will need to break the skin gently with your fingernail, as it can be a little tough.

2 Rub the berry straight onto the paper in a circular motion. Inevitably, some of the blueberry flesh will be left on your page. You may want to remove it so you have just the colour, if you don't want the texture left behind.

3 Here I am using a strawberry cut in half. Rub in a circular motion onto the page using the flat edge of the fruit. The more you swirl, the richer the colour.

A note of caution here: if you use any type of berry, do make sure you wash your hands thoroughly straight after use, especially if you have picked them from the wild. Also, bear in mind that they will stain your fingers.

Blueberries or strawberries from the supermarket are a cheap and accessible way of delving into this area of creativity, especially if you live in an area where country lanes are not easily accessible. You can also use raspberries, sloes, rosehips, blackberries and other wild berries.

The third colour on my page (see right) is produced by a blackberry. It gives a much deeper colour than the strawberry.

This is an example of where I used berries to add colour to a journal page. I used strawberry across the top of the page and blueberry down the right edge. Although blueberries have blue/purple skin, their flesh is usually pale green, and the juice dries to a fairly light shade of blue.

Leaf imprints

Do you remember your schooldays of using wax crayons to make leaf rubbings, which produced the most wonderful patterns? I have always loved using leaves. They make the most beautiful rubbings on both paper and cloth. Simply place the leaf under the paper or cloth and rub over the top with a crayon turned on its side, or a coloured pencil.

Try using different leaves as they have fallen off the tree. The more 'leathery' the texture, the better the result. Some good ones to try are horse chestnut, beech and oak leaves.

Dried leaves and petals

You can use dried leaves and petals for all kinds of craft projects, or just keep them as little reminder keepsakes in your journals. Simply press them between the pages of an old book and when completely flat and dry, glue them down very carefully or stitch them onto cloth using normal sewing thread and an oversew stitch.

They will be very delicate and may crumble a little, but they will add a lovely layer of memories to your projects.

Twigs

You can never have enough twigs, in my opinion. Collect them as you go on your daily walks and keep them in unlidded jam jars.

Longer sticks can be used for sewn or woven wall hangings (see right) and add a beautiful rustic element to your collage designs. They are also perfect for introducing younger crafters to the joy of weaving by wrapping threads around the twigs.

Adding colour to cloth and thread

I am often asked about adding colour into a project when using threads for surface stitching or patterns on plain cloth. How do you combine them? How do you add extra colour? These questions can send people into a complete spin.

Mother Earth knows the secret of blending colours, textures and tones together in a wonderful way that always seems to work perfectly. So for that reason, I love to use natural dyes in my work whenever I can, especially when using a natural or plain cloth as a background.

There are a variety of ways to include natural colours in your creative projects. Here are two of my favourites to get you started.

Solar dyeing

This is a wonderful way of collecting natural dyes for adding to your little cloth snippets. It is also a really easy process that the whole family can get involved in, so it's a perfect project for those summer holiday months when the children are off school.

You will need a clean empty jam jar with a lid, a handful of cotton or lace snippets and a handful of berries.

+ Fill your jam jar three-quarters full of tepid water.
+ Add the berries and cloth snippets.
+ Put the lid on securely, then shake a little to mix the ingredients together.
+ Place on a windowsill that catches the sunlight and leave for at least two weeks.
+ Give the jar a little shake each day.
+ After two to four weeks, remove the cloth remnants and allow to dry naturally on a washing line.

These cloth snippets are then ready to be sewn into a project. They will not be colourfast, so make sure it is a project you know will not be laundered.

Note: if you see any mould forming in your jar, make sure you discard the contents and start afresh. These hiccups will occur, and it isn't something you will have done. It is simply what can happen when you use fresh ingredients, so don't let it put you off trying again.

| *Marigolds:* 1 day | *Blueberries:* 1 week | *Blackcurrants:* 1 week | *Strawberries:* 2½ weeks | *Marigolds:* 2 weeks | *Rose campion:* 2 weeks |

Creating your own natural dyes

This is a real favourite of mine. You can use a variety of different options taken from a wealth of natural ingredients. Once you start experimenting you will want to try anything and everything. Here are a few suggestions:

+ Vegetables: onion skins, red cabbage, carrot tops
+ Leaves: nettles
+ Spices: turmeric

Below I have shown an easy starting point using brown onion skins. I collect these as I peel them when cooking and save them until I have a big enough collection to use. There are no specific quantities given. Just experiment and have fun. However, please remember that, because we have not used a fixative, the dyed cloth will not be colourfast.

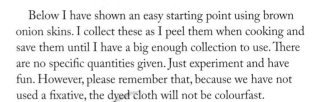

1 Place some water in a saucepan and slowly bring to the boil.

2 Place a generous quantity of onion skins in the saucepan and turn off the heat.

3 Using a pair of tongs, swirl the skins around to make sure each one is fully submerged. Allow them to steep for at least an hour or so. The longer you leave them, the deeper the colour.

4 Using the tongs, remove all the skins from the saucepan and discard. You now have some coloured dye to use.

5 If the liquid is cold, heat it gently so that it is tepid. Place the pieces of cloth you want to dye into the warm onion water. I used a piece of dry calico.

6 Make sure the cloth is fully submerged, turning it over several times to soak up the water and get an even coverage.

7 Leave the cloth in the water for at least two hours. You will see the colour change in front of your eyes. If you can bear the wait, leave it overnight to see how the colour deepens.

The example above shows how leaving your cloth in the dye for longer creates a richer hue. The piece on the left was soaked overnight, while the piece on the right was left for three days. Dry the cloth thoroughly before use. Please remember that, because we have not used a fixative, the dyed cloth will not be colourfast.

Tip

If you wet the cloth before putting it into the saucepan, you will usually get a richer colour.

You can also use your dyed water as a paint wash on paper, although you do have to be careful of mould forming if you leave the liquid too long after you have created it. Here I have used the orangey-brown water from boiling the onion skins to add colour to a design in one of my journals. The colour may fade eventually to a dull sepia tint, but I think that is the magical aspect of using such dyes.

Here I used a little boiled nettle water to add to a finished journal wrap in order to create a deeper shade among the greenery of my cloth. I will then stitch over it with green threads to complete my design.

I love the fact that a little natural magic is nestled in among the threads of my stitched collage. For me, it completes the circle of all the ingredients mixing together beautifully.

46

Here are few examples of different variations. You can see that different pieces of cloth will absorb the dye much more intensely than others. The same principal applies to lace and trims. The general rule is that the more natural the fibre, the richer the colour. Sari silk, calico and yarns are lovely to work with, as they can produce some gorgeous deeper shades.

Moving on to cloth and thread

Whenever I design a project, I always need a story behind it to help me complete the process. Not everyone is the same, but that is an important element of my work. This is where my journals become invaluable to me. I use the inspirations stored between each page as my starting point. Allow your mind to wander as you meander your way through your journals. Memories will magically appear as little reminders, and you may get a little sidetracked at times, but follow your train of thought, as this is part of your creative process.

Write down your thoughts as you may capture ideas to include later. You might take what seems like hours just fiddling and faffing with cloth, choosing threads and thinking of all the other elements you want to add to your mix. Embrace it! This is the beautiful part of creative serendipity.

The next step is to start gathering all the exciting ingredients you will need to begin creating. For me, most projects seem to evolve organically over time, so an idea may not finish in exactly in the way it was envisaged at the beginning.

A few things to ask yourself:
✦ Are the pieces of cloth the right size?
✦ Are they situated in the right spot?
✦ Have you chosen the right cloth to stitch?
✦ Would you prefer to create your own dyed cloth?
✦ What snippets do you wish to add?

I am always saying 'allow the cloth to talk'. What do I mean by that? Well, a vintage piece of cloth will never look pristine. It may be warped or crinkled. You may like the pattern for your project but feel it is bare and may need covering with embellishments. You may dislike the newness of your cloth and wish to 'dull' it to suit your project.

I choose a project based on the colour or pattern of the cloth, then select the threads to match. I then decide on techniques I want to include, and match them all together slowly as I start to create.

1 Start small and lay out your pieces of cloth to see how they look together. Remember that at this early stage you will be creating a base to sew upon, so your colours may eventually blend into the background and not be as prominent as you think they may look initially.

2 Use simple running stitches to sew your patches together. If you wish this to be part of your design you could add more embroidery stitches.

3 Build up the layers of ingredients gradually by putting them together, moving elements around and testing which items work together, before you start stitching.

While dabbling with a few ideas, I ended up using a vintage image overlaid onto one of my own photographs. I then doodled onto the paper print to finish my design.

I developed my idea by printing the photograph onto a piece of silk using an inkjet printer and stitching over the top with some surface embroidery to create a sewn collage. The beautiful mix of silk and cotton creates a gorgeous soft backdrop to sew onto.

This piece was created for a National Lottery-funded project showcasing 'Memories from Days Gone By' at a local museum.

In this example, I drew directly onto kitchen paper, which was dyed with a teabag to create a vintage look. It was then hand sewn onto a collage created by combining vintage papers and cotton to form a base, before adding silk flower snippets taken from an old blouse with a little free motion embroidery on top. This piece was created for an exhibition depicting the beauty of the Fens during wintertime.

ESSENTIALS FOR SLOW STITCHING

Cloth

I like to work with a whole host of options when it comes to cloth, from new to old to vintage to antique. I love exploring the different thicknesses, patterns and types of weave available, although vintage cloth is, of course, my ultimate go-to choice! Below is a list of some of my favourites.

Cottons   Vintage pillowcases, floral prints, block-printed pieces and traditional chintzes. They are easy to use and very versatile for all kinds of creative projects.

Linens   Tableware, bedlinen, flax, hemp and organics all excite me because of their simplicity and link to our past. They can be adapted to so many designs; painted and drawn on, colour washed or dyed and are perfect for embellishing in some way.

Denim   This is a good base for stitched collages.

Calico   An absolute must to have in your stash. It is great for drawing on, stamping and block printing patterns on too, great for writing labels, designing patterns with and for creating your book wrap or slow-stitched bases.

Hessian   Not the easiest of fabrics to work with due to the fact that it frays, but I love it for the added texture.

Muslin   Great for eco-dyeing, painting and colour washing, as well as embroidering.

Lace and organza   These fabrics add a wonderful beauty of their own, due to their delicate nature.

Silk and satin   You really can't beat these two beauties for adding a real touch of elegance to a design. They are perfect partners for eco-dying and colour washing, especially recycled sari silks, which positively gleam as you work with them.

Tweed/wool/worsted   I adore working with these treasures. They lend a gorgeous soft texture to any project.

Velvet   The ultimate in luxury, but it can sometimes be a tricky character to work with. Don't be put off, though – it will reward you with its beauty.

A note on threads

I love to dabble with all kinds of threads when I sew. I am drawn by the colour, texture and beauty of a thread, rather than the actual use and so, as a result, I mix and match and see what happens. I also love to combine old vintage threads with beautiful new silks, alongside some unusual others such as 2-ply wool, tapestry yarn, cotton silks and crochet cottons. A selection of some of my favourites are shown above. I have a number of vintage Sylko threads in my collection, which are lovely to work with and the colour range is beautiful. They also blend very well with all kinds of vintage cloth.

Below is an example of running stitch worked in a variety of threads from simple sewing thread to aran-weight yarn. You can see the variation in thickness and texture. It is always a good idea to keep little swatches like this to refer back to, and help you decide which threads you like working with the most.

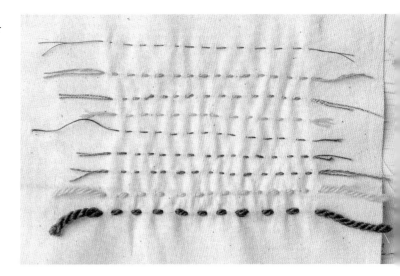

Embellishments

Embellishments are simply little adornments to add to any creative project. Many people think it just means buttons or beads, but there is so much more to add to your designs. Anything that adds an extra layer of loveliness to a project is a winner, in my opinion. So here are a few suggestions:

✦ Buttons and beads
✦ Vintage gems such as pearls, Bakelite buttons and crystal sparkles

✦ Old jewellery, brooches and broken snippets of glittery bling
✦ Coins, keys and mementoes
✦ Paper labels and tickets
✦ Snippets of trims, ribbons and sari silks
✦ Suffolk puffs
✦ Crocheted flowers and knitted leaves
✦ Millinery flowers
✦ Doilies, lace and silks
✦ Found objects such as shells, pebbles, leaves and twigs.

Sewing equipment

I'm often asked what sewing equipment I use and my answer is always the same. Find out what makes you smile, just like the pens and sketching items. If you don't enjoy using something, you will never enjoy your craft and the same goes for sewing equipment. You only need a basic set of items to get started. I've listed some of my essentials below.

Scissors   Invest in a good pair of sharp embroidery scissors for the fine detail and a dressmaking pair for all your heavy work. You will also need a separate pair for cutting paper.

Needles   I like to use a good selection to accommodate all the different thicknesses of my threads. They don't have to be expensive ones either. Find your favourites and keep them separate so they are easy to find.

Pins   Make sure you keep a mixed box handy to use with all the different textures you will be using. If you are intending to use some pins for paper, keep these separate because they will become blunt over time and may damage your cloth if you are swapping between the two.

Pincushion   This is an essential piece of my sewing kit.

Tape measure/ruler   Both of these items are handy to have with you.

Rotary cutter and self-healing cutting mat   Essentials for any sharp, accurate cutting.

Air-erasable marker pen   I use these all the time. They are brilliant for drawing onto cloth before starting a design. Bear in mind that they do erase quite quickly, though.

Safety pins   These are perfect for adding an extra pair of hands into the equation when fixing things together.

Fusible webbing   This interfacing adheres two pieces of cloth together simply by ironing. There are many different brands available but they all do basically the same thing. I use this mainly in appliqué work if I need an accurate finish, and always keep a stash handy just in case an old piece of cloth needs a little extra support when sewing onto it. It is perfect for vintage cottons.

Paper for patterns   I often use brown paper for my designs, but any type of paper can be used. It is a good way to recycle leaflets that come through the post.

Embroidery hoop   I don't use these very often as I like to feel the cloth through my fingers as I slow stitch a project, but there are times when you need a little extra support if you are working with a tricky piece of cloth.

STARTING TO STITCH

By now I'm sure you must be itching to get started, and your head must be full of ideas and inspirations to get going. So how do you use your lovely doodles and collected pieces and put them into a project? The secret is always to start small. Work on little patches of cloth and combine them into projects. You can draw straight onto cloth, or do some hand stamping on it if you need help to get started. Below are some extra techniques that will help with creating your projects.

Joining pieces of cloth together

If I am hand sewing, I prefer to use running stitch to join pieces of cloth together, as it's the simplest and easiest solution, but it depends on the project. If you want a stronger finish, you may wish to backstitch your pieces together, or even machine sew them.

Running stitch

This is one of the oldest methods of attaching one piece of cloth to another (see right). You can create so much with such a simple technique. The key is to make sure your stitches are secure at the beginning and end of each line of sewing (see page 123).

Backstitch

Backstitch creates a firmer bond than running stitch, especially if you use a thicker thread such as cotton perle to secure your work, but you need to think carefully – don't waste your luxurious thread on backstitching.

See Tilly's Stitchery on pages 118–125 for details on embroidery stitches used in this book.

A marriage of cloth and paper

This is an area of textile art or design that can be a huge worry for some. Combining paper and cloth together is frowned upon by some people, but for me the two make a beautiful marriage.

You can either choose to draw or write onto paper then stitch onto cloth or reverse them to produce a different effect. Hand sewing them together can be a little tricky as the paper can sometimes tear as you sew, but I like to welcome those little blips. If you think it may be too troublesome, why not try sewing a few examples with your machine first?

Surface stitching

What is surface stitching? You hear this phrase all the time in textile work and it is often confused with embroidery. For me, surface stitching is something that adds texture, pattern and softness. It is not necessarily a beautiful finished design, such as an embroidered tablecloth – that is completely different. Surface stitching is adding the bark to a tree design, a few petals in among the grass, or a prominent detail on a piece of raw edge appliqué. It can be hand or machine sewn, woven or even embellished with extras.

It can be an overlay of an 18th century floral design on a modern piece of cloth, or a snippet of 19th century lace sewn over a felted scarf. It's simply about a beautiful, tactile explosion of loveliness.

Above I have combined a mix of paper and cotton cloth to begin with, and then added lots of straight stitches to create more texture and cover the joins.

Seed stitch, shown above, is a great way to join cloth pieces together and create some continuity between them. (See also page 124.)

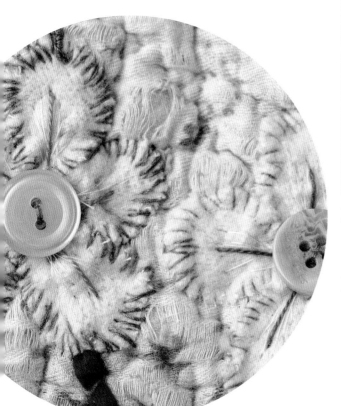

In this example (see left) I combined a little raw appliquéd felt for softness onto a piece of gorgeously crinkly aged antique quilt. The result is a beautiful combination.

Crazy patchwork

Crazy patchwork evolved a long time ago from the necessity of saving cloth scraps from much-loved but worn-out garments; nothing was wasted. The scraps were used to recreate something beautiful to adorn the home, as exemplified by this Victorian tea cosy I found at an antique fair several years ago (see right). Cloth was treasured much more then, and out of that era came a new style of patchwork. Every piece of cloth had its value. Expensive cloth such as velvets, silks and satins were popular ones to use in Victorian times.

I have always loved crazy patchwork since I discovered it during needlework lessons at school. The nostalgia associated with those golden days of buying and choosing cloth, ribbons and lace from an old-fashioned haberdashery shop, full to the brim with gorgeous colours of cottons and silks, always raises a smile.

But much as I adore the crazy patchwork patterns, I struggle with triangular geometric designs – I like to meander as I stitch, and the traditional crazy patchwork style is a little too angular for me.

So after years of experimenting, I've adapted my own style of crazy patchwork stitching that wanders over the cloth as I work. I use the original designs as inspiration but add my own style of sewing them together. I start with a square or oblong scrap of cloth and build my design slowly, tacking each piece down with sewing thread and building up the layers with different textures (see below left and right).

I then let the threads meander over the design like an old-fashioned honeysuckle or rambling rose. I mix and match colours, fabric thicknesses and stitch combinations.

Kantha

Kantha work (meaning 'patched cloth') is a form of Indian folk-art embroidery originating from Bangladesh. It refers to the tradition of slow stitching something useful and beautiful out of discarded or worn-out items – typically sari and muslin cloth – using kantha stitch, which is simply a small, straight running stitch.

Kantha stitching is not only a form of freestyle embroidery, but is also a brilliant way of adding some beautiful surface stitching to any textile art designs. Traditional kantha patched cloths are usually covered in tiny running stitches with beautiful motifs, birds and trees added as decoration using the same thread throughout. I've been drawn to this type of stitching for many years now, as it is similar to the style of patchworking I was used to as I was growing up. This style of recycling was common in the Fens. Many of my ancestors used this technique to save anything and everything in order to make items for their cottages; even old agricultural sacks were used as foundation pieces for bed covers and other items.

I use kantha stitching particularly if I want to add texture to a design by combining a mixture of different threads, colours and thicknesses. I don't worry about the regularity or the evenness of my stitches, as the quirkiness adds a handmade flavour.

In the example above, I experimented with threads in different colours, worked in circles. They provide the background for two pieces of cotton cloth that were joined together.

Here I used a variegated thread that has created a soft swirl of gentle colour as the circular stitching radiates outwards.

In the example above, I experimented with wavy lines, representing the sea, to add texture to a seaside collage.

I rescued this piece of traditional block-printed kantha-stitched quilt (see right) from a factory in Jaipur, which I visited while tutoring on a textile tour in 2020. I adored the combination of colours. I think it tells its own story through the stitching.

Appliqué

'Appliquéd' simply means 'applied' and is a beautiful decorative technique in which a neatly sewn shape is added to a project. Although this method can be worked by machine-sewing using fusible web, I prefer the traditional handsewn method as it gives a much more gentle, handmade look to my work and is the type of sewing our grandmas would have done.

Appliqué allows you a free rein with surface stitching and texturing as you will get frayed edges, puckered lines and textured patches if you wish.

Simply cut out a piece of cloth in the shape you require and sew it onto your slow-stitched collage. I've listed below a couple of ways for securing your cloth.

Turned edge appliqué

This method protects all the raw edges and creates a neat finish. Simply choose your shape and cut it out. Pin it in place on another piece of cloth. To secure it, handsew your shape in place with a small oversew stitch all the way around, tucking the edges under as you sew (see right). Make sure you secure the ends thoroughly as they can easily 'peel' off through wear and tear.

Raw edge appliqué

This method allows you to leave the raw edges showing and lends itself beautifully to wobbly lines and frayed edges (see both examples below).

Pin your cut shape in place. To secure, simply handsew the shape in place with an exaggerated oversew or running stitch. This is particularly good for flowers and leaves.

*Cherish all your happy moments...
they make a beautiful cushion for our old age*

Couching

In embroidery, couching is a technique in which yarns or other materials are laid on the surface of the fabric and fastened in place with small stitches. You can also use it to 'catch down' objects such as sticks, feathers and found objects. Usually, you use a small straight stitch to secure the laid thread or object.

In the example above I used blanket stitch, rather than a straight stitch, to sew down a twig collected from one of my walks. I used the same method (see below) to create a spine on one of my much-loved journals. I love combining them with a variety of different coloured threads.

In the example above, I couched down a vintage green cotton braid with an oversew stitch to create a curlicue on a piece of British wool, and I combined it with a twisted silk ribbon in a contrasting colour.

Finishing off

There are always a few last things that you may like to add to a project. Here are a few suggestions below.

Labels and tags

I love the fact that a little tag can be the finishing sparkle on any design. It not only personalizes and helps with storage, but it also offers you a helping hand when referencing something quickly. In addition, it can preserve the memory of a dear friend, a special visit somewhere or a favourite place.

So, what do you put on a tag? Well, you may want to add names, dates, places, inspiring quotes, keywords, titles or just hand-drawn doodles. Here are a few examples (see right).

Decorative ties

Quite often you will find that your journal will expand quickly, especially if you have a stash of keepsakes inside. I like to keep things simple and just tie my journals with a ribbon or piece of lace to keep all the collected items safely nestled inside. You may also want to use this method if you are creating a stitched wrap, collage or book wrap.

Memorabilia

Adding little extras like photographs, tickets, recipes, collected items or misplaced found objects such as keys, buttons and odd quirky keepsakes can all add to the flavour of a beautiful recipe. All of the above can be added to any project or just saved as keepsakes in your journals.

Not all will withstand the test of time if they are fragile. You may need to protect them a little more by adding organza bags to keep things together, glass bottles for small keepsakes, envelopes for paper items, or you could create fabric pockets for any additional pieces just by sewing a running stitch around three of the edges.

Tip
✦ Safety pins, paper clips and glue are useful things to keep on hand for securing extra items into your projects.

Below is an example of my haberdashery journal of keepsakes. I love to keep adding to it, even though it is a completed project.

I often add little extras to the edges of my collages or cloth journals. The example below is one such journal.

The Projects

Gatherings

I started keeping an annual nature diary, inspired by Edith Holden's writing, several years ago and it is still one of the things that makes me happiest. Each January I start a fresh one.

I love that each one is different and lives its own life, eventually becoming a little heirloom in itself, capturing my thoughts, my walks, and all the beautiful snippets of nature that I collect throughout each season. Some are full to the brim with information and others are sometimes empty where my entries have dwindled due to work or family commitments, but I love them all equally.

I like to give each journal a cover; it gives them an individuality by reflecting their contents and provides peace of mind, knowing that my little gems are all safely nestled inside a cosy book wrap.

I usually work on the wrap at the same time as adding to the contents; that way I am able to marry the two together as I create and design. I really enjoy the slow process of building up layers of cloth and embellishments to create a textured collage. It's a very gentle but thought-provoking process as I try and use all kinds of items, found objects and embellishments I stumble across on my travels.

'Gatherings' is an example of a journal wrap depicting my love of trees and woodlands, and the magic they hold for me. As this one took several months to create, sadly I can't replicate that here, but I will explain the process so you can create something similar. I hope it will inspire you to start stitching.

Finished size

Approximately 18 x 24cm (7 x 9½in)

What you need

Shop-bought or handmade journal
Calico for the foundation
A selection of base fabrics, including vintage clothing, if desired
Memorabilia and other items to personalize the journal
Needle and selection of threads

You can use these ideas in other projects too. I created my wrap from a foundation base of calico (see page 33) and layered on a few patches of cloth that had a woodland theme. I then added all kinds of embroidery stitches as surface stitching to create a more textured look.

When creating your own version, you may like to keep on adding to your design as the year progresses. In doing so, your project may evolve into something completely different from the initial ideas you started with at the beginning of the year. Go with it.

Creating your journal wrap

First of all, make a foundation base out of calico following the instructions on pages 33–35. Then decorate it using the process described here. I have used an alternative version to my original using different pieces of cloth to show you how to get started. You can see how gathering a lovely selection of different pieces of cloth will help create a depth as a starting point for your base (see below left).

1 Place a mixture of different fabric patches onto your calico base and pin them in place.

2 Next layer any raw edge appliqué pieces on top of the patches to add more detail. You can be quite experimental by snipping into the cloth pieces to create extra depth that will help to build up your design.

3 Add even more depth to your appliqué pieces by 'teasing out' the raw edges with a needle to fray them.

Once you are happy with the base, then you can start on the really creative part of the project. Some examples are shown below.

4 Paint on a little colour wash for extra richness.

5 Add a little surface stitching and embroidery, such as seed stitch and feather stitch, for texture.

6 Here I have worked a blanket stitch edging to neaten the raw edges.

7 Embellishments such as pearls or beads can now be sewn onto edges.

8 Don't forget to make a feature of the spine by sewing on ribbons and buttons – they are a wonderful combination.

This is a variation on my design, made using different fabrics.

9 Finally, tie a long strip of cloth round your journal to secure it and protect the contents and memorabilia. You don't want to lose all those treasures you've collected.

This shows the reverse of my Gatherings journal. I used a lovely green leaf button as extra decoration on the cord tie.

Here you can see some content from my journal, showing memories from my walks and how the found objects have inspired my sketches.

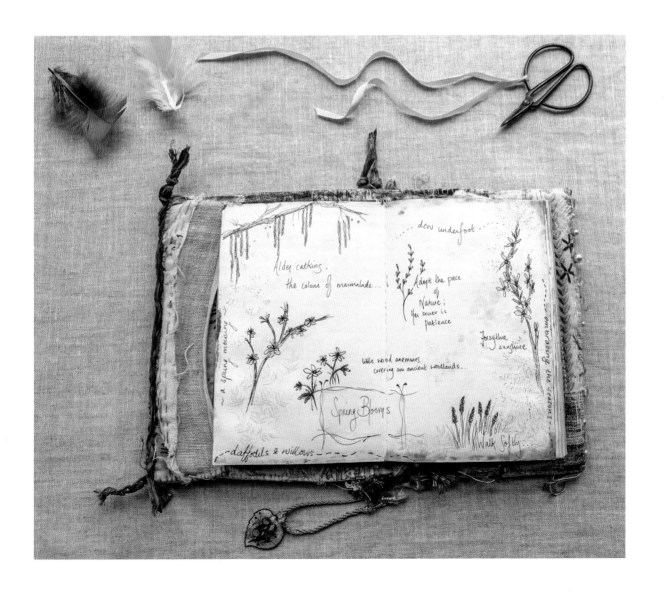

Diary of a Fen Gal

This project focuses on creating your own paper journal to take with you while out walking on your daily rambles. I want to show you how to make one of my own 'rustic style' paper journal designs that I have been creating since I was a little girl and still love to make to this day.

As a young child I would make these with any scrap paper that I could find to create little books for my dolls when playing schools. This version is obviously a more adult, decorated design that I hope will inspire you to make one for yourself. They are perfect companions when you don't want to carry a heavy book around, and they are great for children during school holidays.

I often use paper journals for collecting and pressing flowers and foliage while out walking, as well as doodling ideas that I use later as inspiration for stitched designs. I like to create a size that fits snugly inside one of my dockey bags (see the project on page 110).

This project was initially inspired by the vastness of the Fenland skies where I live, and the fabulous hues they offer to visitors, especially during the summer months, when they are renowned for their outstanding sunsets. I love capturing the heritage, social history and beauty of the countryside that surrounds me whenever I can in colour, pattern or texture.

Our part of the country was once known as the 'agricultural basket of England' due to the textured patchwork of rich agricultural fields which were exceptionally productive. These fields were filled with labourers, some of whom were my ancestors. They toiled the land day and night, often in harsh conditions, to get fresh produce picked and ready for markets the next day. I often heard my aunts and uncles say that the only elements that surrounded them during their week were the wide open skies of sunshine, clouds and wild winds.

Finished size

Approximately 15.5 x 22cm (6 x 8¾in)

What you need

A selection of around six papers of any thickness and colour; I used handmade A4 (210 x 297mm/8¼ x 11¾in) paper for extra texture

A4 piece of calico for cover

Acrylic fabric paints

Paintbrush

Selection of hand stamps

Glue stick

Ink pen (optional)

1m (1yd) of lace or ribbon to tie the pages together

Creating your journal

I show you here how I created the original calico background design, but also offer a couple of variations on the finishing techniques to give you a different option if you wish to experiment. You can choose how thick you want to make your books by changing the number of sheets you use. In general, I like to use five A4 (210 x 297mm/8¼ x 11¾in) sheets of paper folded in half to create the pages, and one extra sheet for the outer cover. You can use whatever size paper suits you.

1 Lay all the sheets of paper on top of each other in a landscape orientation, then fold them all in half (not shown). Don't worry about getting a sharp fold – this isn't important. Remove the first one, as this will form the cover when combined with your calico colour wash.

2 To make the cover, lay your calico on a plastic tray or glass mat to protect your work surface, as the paint will soak through the fabric. Get your paints together with the colours you want to use, a brush and a pot of water. I used acrylic paints here for a vibrant effect, but if you want subtle tones, watercolours are a better option.

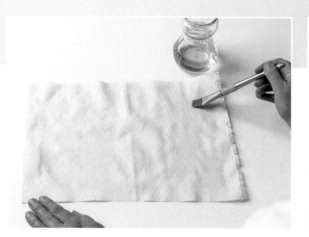

3 Wet the paintbrush using warm water and brush it over the calico. Give it a few minutes to soak into the cloth, but don't oversaturate it. You only want to make it wet enough to soak up some of the paint.

4 Once the cloth is damp, gradually start adding your colours to the cloth with the paintbrush.

5 Experiment by making some areas stronger in colour than others to create areas of interest. Add more water if you feel the fabric needs it.

6 Allow the colours to bleed and merge into each other, creating a beautiful symphony of shades. When you have finished, let the calico dry on a sheet of newspaper or, if it is a sunny day, you can leave it outside to dry.

7 Once the calico is dry, the colours will be a little more subdued. The frayed edge on the right is something that I regard as a design feature, but you can neaten your edges if you prefer.

Finishing your journal

8 Once your painted calico is dry you can stick it to your outer paper cover with a glue stick. Apply glue all around the edges and the centre of the paper to cover the page evenly.

9 Carefully place the outer paper page down centrally onto the wrong side of the painted calico.

10 Press the paper page down firmly so that it sticks securely.

11 Next, place the paper pages inside your cover. Align the centre folds made in step 1.

12 Use a piece of lace or ribbon to wrap round the centre of the pages.

13 Tie it in a bow or a knot to secure it.

14 Add some decorations. Here I am using one of my own rubber stamp designs – a favourite motto of mine that I have attached to an acrylic block. I love to add words when I can, and build up the design around them.

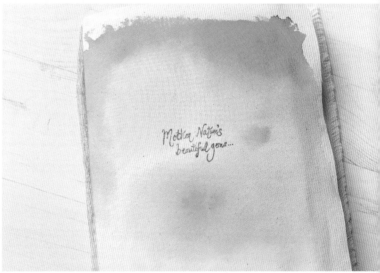

15 Allow the stamp to dry for a few minutes so that you don't smudge it.

Tips

✦ You may want to create all your pages using the same method as for the cover if you are using plain white paper, to make it extra special.

✦ If you use handmade papers, you will add a much more tactile feel to your work. Handmade papers are softer than commercially bought paper, which makes flower squishing or pressing a much more gentle process.

16 When you've finished stamping, you can draw leaf motifs with an ink pen.

Below is my finished cover. The leaf design was inspired by a neem tree that I saw while visiting Jaipur, India. I love it as it is so similar to all the willow trees we have surrounding the Fen wetlands. I kept this design quite simple in my choice of colours, but you may wish to use a richer palette and add more to yours.

In my original design (see left and page 71) you can see how I experimented by adding some stamped text onto the back of my journal, which gives a lovely nostalgic feel of an old manuscript to the finished design.

Below you can see that I kept the piece of kitchen paper I used when pressing a daffodil into one of my other journals, simply because I loved the imprint so much. I never throw anything away! It can now be used as an extra page at the back of my little Fen diary.

Meandering Paths

Although my home is in the Fens, I love to escape every now and then to our little vintage caravan, affectionately known as Lottie, that nestles on the north Norfolk coastline. While there, I spend some time switching off from a busy lifestyle, reconnecting with nature for a few treasured long walks along the beach and marshlands, through woodlands or simply meandering along the Norfolk lanes. This project was inspired by some of those walks.

I wanted to have a weekend journal travel kit with me to allow me to do some slow stitching while on the move, or to accompany me on days out, without taking a mountain of stuff with me. So I came up with the idea of a journal booklet that enabled me to capture the natural beauty around me, which also contained a little portable sewing kit.

I designed it in such a way that there are no fixed dimensions, so you can determine the overall size of your notes, the quantity of pages and the finished design on the outer cover yourself, to make it suit your own requirements.

The best bit about creating this project was rummaging through my stash choosing colours and patterns to mix into the delicious collage; choosing strips mainly for their textures, their rarity or simply because they smiled back at me. I hope you have just as much fun as I did!

Finished size

Approximately 17 x 25cm (6¾ x 9¾in)

What you need

Five sheets of watercolour paper from an A4 (210 x 297mm/8¼ x 11¾in) sketchpad

A4 piece of bonded interlining (outer cover lining)

A4 piece of printed cotton/linen (inner cover lining)

A4 piece of old blanket or something similar (inner page for sewing essentials)

13 x 18cm (5 x 7in) piece of tweed or old blanket with pinked edges

Selection of frayed, ripped cloth or lace ribbon strips

A lace or ribbon strip for tying the layers together

A selection of stranded cotton embroidery thread or cotton perle thread

Embellishments such as buttons, beads, sequins and tassels (optional)

Creating your book wrap

If you wish your pages to be coloured, stamped or painted, then you will need to do this before assembling your booklet using any of the techniques mentioned earlier in the Techniques and Working with Mother Earth sections (pages 24–47).

When you are happy with the finished pages, fold each one over to create a crease in the middle before assembling. This will make it easier. In this example, I have used a selection of various papers to offer a choice of different options.

1 Start by placing your bonded interlining flat on a surface, cotton side up (RS). This is the foundation base that will create your outer cover design. Start adding the cloth and ribbon strips in any vertical pattern that you like. Spend some time jiggling them about, working out your happiest design. You can use a mix of different fabric weights to create a lovely sea of textures.

2 When you are happy with the position of your cloth strips, pin each piece to the interlining at the top and bottom of each strip and start sewing them on using running stitch and your chosen embroidery threads.

3 When you have sewn all the strips on, the interlining will be covered.

Tip

If you allow the cloth to move slightly as you work, it will settle into its own position. It doesn't matter if your line of stitching isn't straight. The running lines represent your walks, so think of your little rambles as you sew, and allow your thread to wander over the cloth.

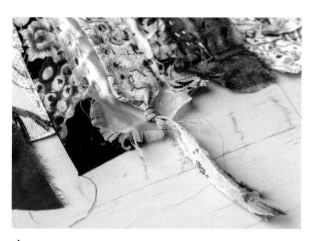

4 If I have any particularly long pieces of cloth, I often tie a knot in the end for a bit of extra texture and decoration.

5 Turn your work over and pin the inner piece of printed cloth to the interlining, with the right side facing up.

6 Attach the piece of cotton by working a line of running stitch around the edges. This will cover the back of your work. I have left the edges frayed, but if you don't like this finish, simply turn them under as you sew the pieces together.

7 Next, lay your completed outer cover flat on a surface with the right side facing down. Place the piece of blanket down on top, but do not attach or sew them together. Then place the piece of pinked tweed or blanket on the left side of the large blanket piece and add your sewing pins and needles to hold it in place.

8 Next, lay your pre-folded pages on top. You are creating a sandwich of layers, so you may wish to change your design to suit. I gave my pages a colour wash with some diluted red wine beforehand.

9 Wrap the length of lace around the pages along the centre line. Close your booklet and tie the lace at the bottom with a crossover tie (as if you were tying your shoelaces) to bind the layers together. You are basically creating a tied spine with the lace.

11 Your can add items to your sewing kit at the front and also embellish your pages with doodles, words and phrases.

10 Your booklet is complete at this stage, but you may wish to add embellishments such as buttons, beads or appliqué to the cover to strengthen the design.

Tip

Don't tie the lace too tightly, as you may wish to add some more pages at a later stage. If you would like to do this, simply slide in a couple more pages through the centre page under the tied lace ribbon.

You may want to stick an envelope onto one of the paper pages for storing a few pens and pencils for drawing, or for collecting a few leaves as you walk.

Take your booklet when you go out for walks and enjoy a little doodle here and there; capture a few leaves between the pages or glue in some flowers or sticks.

An Alchemy of Secrets

From a young age, I was always asking questions: 'Why?', 'What if...?', 'How does it...?', 'What then?'. Call it curiosity, showing an interest, or just downright nosiness but, as a child, I was always being told by teachers not to ask so many questions. Sadly (or happily I like to think), I have still not learnt that skill – even at the ripe old age of 50-something! Having worked in the education sector for over 35 years, I still feel it is important to continually question, learn new things and make discoveries, whatever age we are. As children, we never really think about questioning, we just do things instinctively in a playful way; but as adults, fears and doubt creep into our creative process, which takes away that wonderful world of magical 'wows!' This in turn can hold us back from trying something new, simply to find out what may happen if we dare to try.

Why am I saying all this? When I am eco-dyeing cloth, most of the time my attempts are experimental 'what ifs'. Some days I just dye for the sake of enjoying the delights that brings, and on others there is a purpose to my experiments. I keep a separate journal to record my likes and dislikes, times of day I work, ingredients I've used and notes on any mishaps that occur. I never know how an old piece of lace will react to the dye I am using, whether a piece will be able to take a natural dye and, of course, there is the worry of making something look worse than before I started!

So, my advice is simple. Let serendipity guide you. Allow her to hold your hand as you work, and your creations will evolve organically. Keep a record in your journal and allow all those secrets you discover as you work to stay safe in a special place.

I called this project An Alchemy of Secrets because it was inspired by all the loveliness of that wonderful world of discovery; the world of alchemy. An alchemist is said to be 'a person who transforms or creates something through a seemingly magical process' – and dabbling with dyes in a creative stitched project is a great way of practising your own form of alchemy. Here, I show you how to create a journal wrap for all your notes using beautiful pieces of eco-dyed cloth you create, but you can also adapt this method to use as a foundation for a stitched collage, small wall hanging, or even a special keepsake card using ribbons and lace.

Finished size

Approximately 16 x 23cm
(6¼ x 9in)

What you need

A shop-bought journal of any size and type

Piece of calico for the book wrap

Selection of strips of eco-dyed cloth, ribbon and lace

Handstamped cloth snippets (optional)

Decorative buttons (optional)

Selection of vintage embroidered linens for appliqué (optional)

Glue stick and pins

Daisies Bloom

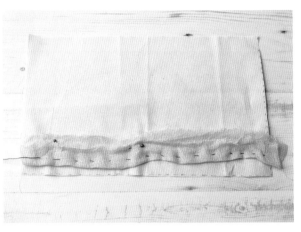

1 Start by creating a cover for your journal with the calico, following the instructions on pages 33–35. Lay your journal flat and open it fully onto the calico. allowing at least 10cm (4in) of excess fabric all around the journal. This is the base onto which you will stitch.

2 Lay out your first strip of cloth onto the calico and pin it in place, then stitch it down. You can use a matching or contrasting colour of thread. I stitched mine down in a horizontal design, using a large tacking stitch.

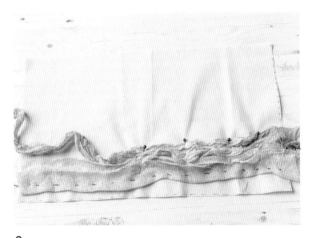

3 Pin down your second length of cloth or ribbon and stitch that on. The effect of the frayed edges is what contributes to the overall sense of texture in this project. Allow the ends of the cloth strips to extend beyond the edges of the calico.

4 Keep adding each new strip close to the previous one so it rests against it snugly. Let the lines flow organically – they should not be straight lines. As far as colours go, my intention was to create a beautiful riverside scene, but I also incorporated the wonderful textured ripples of the wicker basket that I keep all my dyed cloth in (see above left).

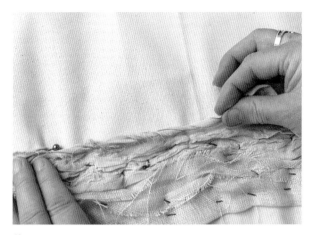

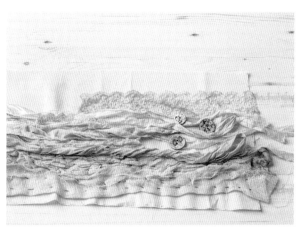

5 To add to the sense of texture, simply twist the cloth strips every now and then as you place them onto the backing cloth, pin and then sew them in place.

6 Incorporate some lace if you have any, to introduce yet another dimension to the texture, and try placing some colourful buttons on top to see how they would look.

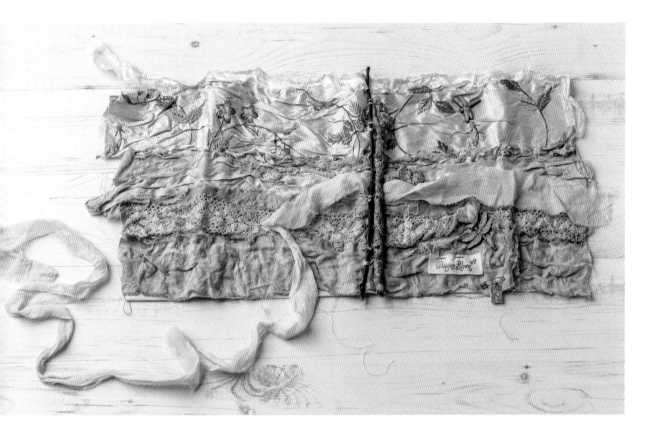

Once the lengths of cloth are sewn down in place, you may like to add some extra embellishments from the things you find or use during your eco-dyeing experiments. Have fun dabbling. For my project, I used a combination of scrim (a light cotton gauze), cheesecloth, sari silk and lace, all of which I had eco-dyed beforehand. The sari silk has

a beautiful sheen, which contrasts with the matt nature of the other fabrics, and adds to the richness of the texture. I also attached some twigs using couching stitches to form the spine of the cover, and a piece of handstamped cloth. Then I threaded a long strip of yellow fabric underneath the twigs so that I could tie my journal shut with a bow.

As well as making notes in my journal on eco-dying experiments, I also keep lots of pieces of eco-dyed cloth and separate sheets of paper in it. For that reason, I deliberately leave the edges of my journal wrap unsewn, to allow it to expand to fit the contents (see above).

Keeping records of your eco-dyeing experiments is very useful as you will be able to refer back to them for colour, ingredients used and so on, when choosing what to include for future projects (see below). Here, I have glued in a piece of 1970s lace for safekeeping after solar dyeing it. You can see that I included information on how long I left the lace in the jam jar.

Here I used a dye of dandelion petals to dip my vintage doily into and added a doodle alongside to remind me of the flower I had used (see above). Your notes really don't have to represent a school workbook. Eco-dyeing is a creative process, so allow your notes to reflect your thoughts in the same way.

My journal is aleady overflowing with thoughts, ideas, techniques, experiments and samples, but I think there is space for just one more...

Tales from a Victorian Haberdashery

Finished size

Approximately 13 x 15cm (5 x 6in)

What you need

A selection of all kinds of cloth snippets of any size, texture or pattern (I used a selection of woollen tweeds but any cloth you have will work equally well)

14.5 x 26.5cm (5¾ x 10½in) piece of green felt

13 x 24.5cm (5 x 9¾in) piece of cream felt for the base

Two 13 x 20cm (5 x 8in) pieces of cream or beige felt for the pages

A selection of embroidery threads, old and new, if you have them

Decorative buttons and beads (optional)

Note: you can pink the edges of all the felt pieces first if you wish.

This project shows you how I transfer the inspirations and doodles taken from my journals into an actual project. You can see on my moodboard of inspirations (see page 95) taken from different journals, how I collected snippets of threads and cloth to use as a starting point when choosing colours and textures.

Although the main project here shows how to create a lovely needle case, I hope that by showing you my moodboard I can encourage you to keep those little extras for future reference in your own haberdashery journal.

My needle case evolved from a trio of delights: my love of crazy patchwork, the busyness of a beautiful Victorian haberdashery, and the inspiring patterns found in an old-fashioned Victorian walled garden. My design started with just a little sketch or two (see below) and a few doodles, which you can use in your own projects (see pages 126–127).

1 Begin by starting to lay out the pieces of cloth onto your base felt. You may want yours to be in an organized pattern, but I like to keep mine quite random. Remember that this is forming the background and will eventually blend into a lovely symphony of colour, so don't overthink it.

2 Once you are happy with your arrangement of patterns and colours, pin each piece in place. It's a good idea to take a photo at this point to remind you of the positioning, in case you need to re-arrange any of the pieces, or take some off to stitch others in place.

3 Choose a stitch pattern for each patch and explore different colour options with your threads. I chose to work blanket stitch around the piece of pink tweed (see page 118).

4 Once each patch is sewn down, start adding extra trails of meandering stitches. I laid a piece of patterned linen over the pink tweed and worked feather stitch on top using green thread, which spills over onto the navy patch (see page 120).

Tips

+ If your stitching doesn't look right, you can always unpick it and re-stitch!

+ Allow your stitching to continue onto neighbouring patches of cloth – you don't have to stop where the fabric ends.

5 Now sew your cream base felt centrally onto the larger green felt using your choice of stitch. I used running stitch with red thread so that it is visible for demonstration purposes, but I would normally use a matching thread so that it doesn't show. For the piece shown above, you can see how I have experimented with different colours to work out the stitch patterns for my sewing onto the actual finished piece below.

6 You can continue to add more stitching to build up the layers of texture. As well as blanket stitch, I used chain stitch to create a lovely meandering wavy line, French knots for creating clusters of flowers and lazy daisy stitches as petals. I also used feather and satin stitch to divide some areas into corners like little pockets of flora. In addition, I combined different threads to create beautiful textures and then finished by embellishing with beads on the edges.

You can make the cover as detailed as you like. I wanted to produce a rich-looking cover so I have overlapped the stitching, used vibrant thread colours and also added some fancy buttons at the top.

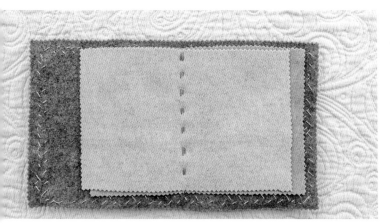

7 The last things to add are the two inner pieces of felt for storing your needles. Sew them down the centre of the opened cover with sewing thread, using running stitch (see above left). Make sure they are slightly offset so that, when you fold them over, you can see each 'page' separately (see above right).

Extra details

I used woven wheel rose stitch (see page 123) to create some flowers (above left) and herringbone stitch to link different pieces of fabric together (above right).

Moodboard of inspirations

You can see here how I love to collect snippets of threads, pieces of cloth, old haberdashery items and other quirky details for future reference. They all nestle inside some form of haberdashery journal that holds a beautiful host of secrets in no particular order, to use as inspiration.

My journals are created from shop-bought notebooks, my own paper designs or handmade cloth journals. I use them as my own little reference library for matching colours, looking at textures, choosing pattern styles or for keeping notes of a preferred embroidery stitch pattern I have used. Of course, you may just like to create a collection of 'stuff' to look at on rainy days. Once you get into the rhythm of creating them, you will be surprised at what you add into the equation. The main thing is to see each page as a source of inspiration that you can keep returning to if you ever need a helping hand in making a creative decision and maybe stroke every now and then – this, as any sewer will know, is the best bit! Most importantly, just have fun with them.

Winter Sparkle

I have been creating stitch wraps for many years now. They can encompass so much or so little, depending on your preference. I can think of nothing better than to stitch all my beautiful inspirations into one whole project and create a really extra-special gem of an heirloom keepsake.

For me, stitch wraps are another way of keeping a visual diary but, instead of doodling on paper, you can doodle on cloth with a combination of inks, threads and embellishments.

They are projects that I never finish, simply because I like to think another generation of sewers could pick up any of mine and start adding more stitching several decades later, to continue the story.

My Winter Sparkle wrap is a tactile, visual diary using cloth and thread that was created in 2019 during the yuletide season. Quite often we think of winter as the season for slowing down and so, for me, a little slow stitching with a cuppa by a warm fire is the perfect combination

for creating a little '*hygge*' smile. This project evolved really slowly as I stitched a little each day while catching up on some of my favourite films, or listening to the radio during the afternoons while watching the Fenland sunset. This wrap introduces you to a lovely way of capturing some special winter moments by creating a tactile, visual diary of designs.

What you need

A foundation base in the size of your choice. Here I have used a piece of calico measuring approximately 1.45m x 25cm (1¾yd x 10in)

Suggestions for materials:
A selection of cloth pieces such as pre-loved cloth, new swatches, charity shop finds or tiny snippets saved from other projects
Cloth with patterns or designs that can be used for raw edge appliqué pieces
Buttons, beads, lace, tassels and ribbons
Memorabilia
Hand-stamped cloth labels or words
A selection of threads

The first thing to do is to make a list of things you see, hear and love about this particular season. I captured all my thoughts about winter and its seasonal delights in a separate journal alongside my sewing, choosing quotes, poems and daily thoughts to guide my stitching, which accompanied my doodles and designs.

Obviously I can't share exactly how I created each element, as it evolved very slowly, but I've given you an outline of how to add some elements to create your design. It actually took me six months to complete the wrap, with my last stitch being sewn while on holiday in June! For me, that's the joy of stitch wraps. There are no rules, no time limits, and you simply can't go wrong with them. They are beautifully meditative in their slowness, creative in their freedom to design and addictive in a cloth and thread kinda way!

I hear so often that the stumbling block to starting any project is where to actually start, so I am hoping, by using this project as a visual aid, that I may be able to persuade some of you to give it a go with your own chosen subject.

The following suggestions are based on creating a similar winter wrap to mine, so you will need to adapt them to suit your own subject matter if you are choosing something different. Make a list of things you see, hear and love about the season. One of the starting points for this project was a treasured tweed scarf that I inherited from my lovely father-in-law, which you can see in the photograph on page 96. From there I collected many snippets of different-sized pieces of cloth with a whole host of different textures, colours and patterns that were similar to form the patchwork base that I created my stitching upon.

Over the next few pages I have shared my tips on creating your own design using your own resources. I must emphasize that, as this project may take a long time to complete, start by taking the pressure off yourself and not committing to an end result. Don't try to picture the finished design at this stage – simply go with the flow.

Gather your inspirations, sketch your designs and start stitching. Once you have added a few stitches to your patches of cloth, you will settle into a gentle rhythm that will even itself out once you get going. Remember that this is your design. If it doesn't quite look right or isn't the right size, or if your stitching is a little wonky, it really doesn't matter. This is your piece of work and no one else's.

Give yourself permission to simply play and create whatever comes to mind, and think of it as a quiet meditation, allowing all the busyness of your day to float away. It doesn't have to make sense in any particular way, it just has to reflect winter in all her glory and sparkle.

Here are a few extra pointers to help you get started with your inspirations:
✦ Make a list of things you wish to include in your project.
✦ Write a list of keywords you wish to embroider, stamp or write on your cloth.
✦ Limit yourself to only five embroidery stitches to avoid an overload of ideas.

The first thing to do is simply gather your stash together and place it in a lovely basket, container or box. Devote something special to your project so that it always accompanies you on your stitching journey. Make it your friend by allowing the cloth and threads that you have chosen to talk to you. I'm always saying this and until you understand how this is totally out of your hands, then you won't relax into your project.

What do I mean by this? Well, you may have chosen an old piece of cloth that has been washed many times or has a grubby stubborn stain and yet it still sings to you because you like the pattern or the grain of your cloth, or it may have been gifted to you by a loved one and you want to include it in your own heirloom piece. It may be warped, caused by many 'ironing Mondays', or it may have a rip in the wrong place, but you still want to include it in your design. Work with it.

Your cloth is talking to you through its threads and own story. Take a few days to keep looking through your collection of items. This may inspire you to go and find extras to add to it, or it may guide you to choose a theme from your selection of materials.

Next, start with a piece of cloth that you like. Decide on a stitch and start sewing, using one of your sketches

or doodles as a starting point. You may wish to cut out a piece of cloth with a pattern or design on it, and use it as an appliqué (see above). Here, I used a printed image of a deer cut from a piece of cotton canvas to sew onto a piece of linen. I then worked feather stitch down the edge, and some straight stitches along the bottom to represent grasses. I added the deer to my design after seeing a herd while out walking at Holkham Hall in Norfolk. It brings back a lovely memory of the day. You can see that I also included some lace to represent the icy nips that filled the Norfolk air!

Here I used a flurry of green seed stitches alongside blanket stitch in a circular pattern to represent the beautiful icy patterns found on my car bonnet one frosty morning. I added a star design created by small straight stitches using a vintage Sylko thread and interlaced it with small snippets of a piece of wedding lace.

You can see below how the overall details meander across the cloth in all directions. I like to turn my cloth around as I sew, and find little pockets of plainness to add details to. I added the words 'Winter Whispers' and 'Imbolc' in backstitch, to lead us from deep winter into spring (Imbolc). By doing this you can date your work and it tells future generations the time of the year I stitched the project.

I love to add little extras to my work that may often have their own story. In the section of the wrap shown above, I used one of my treasured 1930s Suffolk puffs as a small reminder of the lovely hour I spent sorting them into a new basket I had acquired, while watching the snow falling outside. I also added some Indian jingly bells from my stash to remind me that the following winter I would be visiting Jaipur on my textile tour. Little keepsakes often have a deeper meaning to the sewer, but to an observer may just look pretty and they may wonder why that particular item was chosen. It is important to write your story down as you work, if you want to tell future generations about it.

Here you can see that I dated my work using stem stitch with a cotton perle thread. It is at the end of the wrap, so I wound it around a lovely old mill bobbin dating back to the 1950s. The bobbin is useful for storage purposes, but equally it allows me to turn the wrap into a wall hanging if I want to display it at any time.

Allow your trimmings to scatter themselves across your work and simply stitch them down where they lie. I find this a lovely and freeing way of creating designs.

Here, the cotton lace is 'sprinkling' itself over the melody of a sparrow chirping his little heart out in the early morning, as the frost lingers (see right). I stitched onto a piece of early Victorian quilt, which links to the time of year perfectly, but adds a subtle texture at the same time.

I had been saving this gorgeous bunny button (see right) for a special project for ages, and this was the perfect place for it.

Of course, family traditions are a must! Below, my real Christmas tree was added to the design alongside these spirals of wedding lace I found in Paris one holiday. They represent the twinkling lights I love to put up all over our little home at yuletide.

You can see here that I added one of the handmade rolled felted bead decorations, which I created for my Christmas tree. I made one extra to add to my tweed scarf tassel as a little keepsake. It is simply a piece of rolled-up felt stitched together, with beads sewn on as pretty embellishments.

I chose these antique mother-of-pearl buttons because of their original card, as I loved how they sparkle, but they also contrast beautifully against the dullness of the linen and the shimmer of the wedding lace.

I drew a Christmas tree in my journal (see right) before stitching it, in order to work out dimensions and colours.

Alternative project

Although my Winter Sparkle wrap is made purely with stitching, you may like to incorporate some of the other techniques I have shown you in this book, such as painting on cloth, hand-stamping or embellishing. I created the stitch wrap below, which I called 'Jaipur Rainbow of Serendipity', while I was in India. It shows how I added a colour wash as a base, then drew designs straight onto the cloth. With that process done, it is now ready for the stitching to be added.

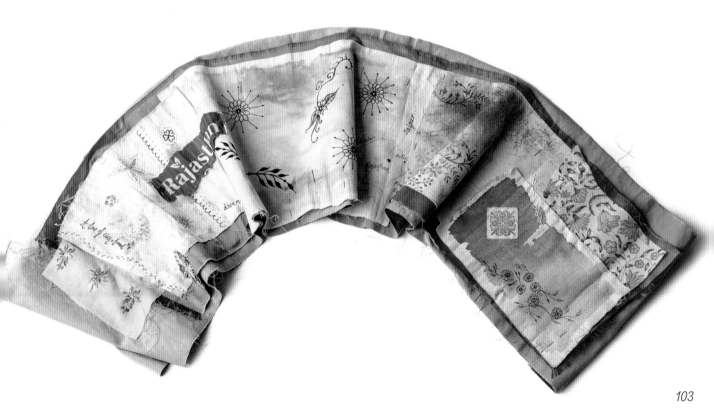

Jar of Smiles

Finished size

Approximately 11 x 30cm (4¼ x 11¾in) not including the jar

What you need

Jam jar
Paper snippets
Calico snippets
Selection of threads
30 x 10cm (12 x 4in) piece of grey felt
26 x 8cm (10¼ x 3in) piece of white felt

25 x 7cm (9¾ x 2¾in) piece of rose-printed cotton fabric
10cm x 4cm (4 x 1½in) piece of torn handmade paper for the label
Four small buttons
Lace for the ties
White cotton perle thread
Pinking shears (optional)
Template for the label (see page 126)

*Please note that I have given measurements for my jam jar to give a rough idea of size. Measure your own jar and adjust the fabric sizes to make sure the wrap reaches around the jar comfortably.

This project is one of the easiest in the book and one of the most exciting, I think. It allows serendipity to guide you.

I am a collector of jam jars – any shape, any size and any colour – and I keep them for all kinds of special items such as buttons, threads and embellishments, but I also love to add words into the equation. This project encourages you to create your own special place to keep all your precious secrets, quotes, memories, sayings or notes tucked safely away in a pretty jar for future use. You may like to create numerous jars, each for different items, or just have one for everything.

If you are collecting memories, you could start your jar at the beginning of the year and fill it gradually. The contents will be a lovely reminder of those treasured family times when you revisit your memories again at Christmas, perhaps as you share a day with beloved family members.

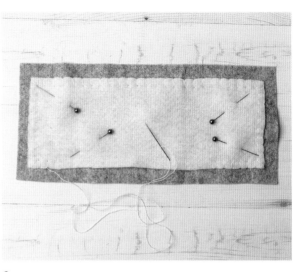

1 Place the grey felt around the jar. It should almost meet in the middle. You need a small gap so that you can tie the buttons together at the end.

2 Lay the rectangle of white felt on top of the grey felt and sew it in place using blanket stitch (see page 118).

3 Next, attach a handwritten label to the centre of the cotton rectangle using running stitch. I've suggested paper (see the photo on page 105) but you could quite easily use a calico label if you prefer, as shown below. Lay the cotton fabric on top of the stitched felt and secure it using running stitch.

4 Using the point of your needle, fray the edges of the printed cotton to give it a fluffy edge. Do this by placing the needle into the raw edge of the fabric and pushing the theads upwards to release them. They will then pull away quite easily.

5 Pink the edges of the grey felt with pinking shears to give a decorative edge, if you wish.

6 Next, add a few embroidered stitches, such as lazy daisies, to soften the edges of the label. I've added a beautiful snowflake in among mine, taken from a piece of 1950s lace. I've used it like a small piece of raw edge appliqué, then embroidered over it with the daisies.

7 Sew the buttons to each end of the grey felt, top and bottom.

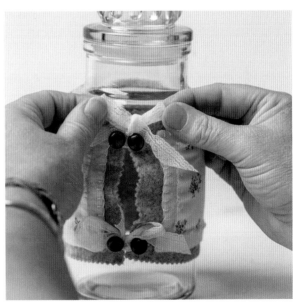

8 Wrap the label around the jar and tie lengths of lace or ribbon around the buttons to secure it. You may also wish to tie a length of lace around the top of the jar.

Fill your jar with whatever items are precious to you. I fill mine with a variety of things, from words and phrases written on scraps of paper, to buttons, beads and scraps of lovely fabric that remind me of something or someone special.

You could also use your jar to collect pieces of jewellery that have a special meaning for you, or shells from beaches you have visited over the years (see right). Perfect for a family project while on holiday!

For this project, I used an old sweet jar from the 1970s that belonged to my Mum, so the jar itself is a memory, as well as the contents.

A Fenland Dockey

Whenever I travel anywhere for a little ramble, I always try to take a journal of sorts, my phone to use as a camera and something to sketch with.

Over the years, I have experimented with all types of bag to house all my little extras, such as a rucksack, holdall, basket and so on, but have never really found anything that suited me. They would either fall off my back as I leant forward to take a photograph, or the straps would make my shoulders ache trying to keep them in place as I moved about.

Nothing seemed to work, so I decided to create my own version. I needed a bag that allowed my hands to remain free, was easily accessible with no zips or ties and wouldn't weigh heavy on my shoulders. The result was an old-fashioned Fenland 'dockey bag'.

A dockey bag was a fenman's go-to bag that he would use to carry his lunch in while working on the land. Agricultural workers would be docked pay if they stopped to take a tea break, so this bag allowed them to take a swig of cold tea from a flask and a mouthful of bread and cheese as they worked in the fields, by having the bag crossed over their shoulders as they worked.

They would all have had their own personal version, sewn by their wives, created from a piece of sacking or agricultural cloth, and stitched together with linen or hemp thread. The design was very plain as it was a functional item, certainly not decorated like mine.

Finished size

Approximately 23 x 28cm (9 x 11in), not including strap

What you need

30 x 70cm (11¾ x 27½in) piece of green linen or cotton outer

30 x 70cm (11¾ x 27½in) piece of beige linen or cotton lining

20 x 25cm (8 x 9¾in) piece of natural linen or cotton

20 x 25cm (8 x 9¾in) piece of deluxe interlining or old blanket

5 x 17cm (2 x 6¾in) piece of lace

3 x 140cm (1¼ x 55in) strip of blanket for the strap

Selection of embroidery threads and yarns in different colours

Embellishments such as buttons, beads and lace (optional)

Coloured pencils

Design inspiration

Initially, my design was for a plain bag using just green and beige linen, which would have been the original colours used by farm workers, but I thought a decorated panel would be a really lovely addition after discovering an embroidered linen bag (shown below) at a local antique fair.

The bag dates from the early 1920s and was used as an afternoon needlework bag for the lady of the house to keep all her sewing items in while she stitched. I loved this idea so much that I included the stitched inspiration in my design by adding a scene from my beloved Fen wetlands using a drawing that I made while out walking on the marshes one day (see bottom left).

I wanted to keep my design quite rustic to represent the links to my past, which is why I left raw edges and allowed it to keep its organic feel with a basic handsewn assembly.

Fen workers were renowned for their ingenuity in creating something out of nothing, purely for practical use. I hope I have done them proud by keeping to their tradition and adding only a little extra stitched embellishment as an added dimension.

To create your panel

1 First, lay the natural linen piece on top of the deluxe lining. Then you can start stitching. I used some green wool yarn to create a series of straight stitches of different lengths. Then I worked some lines of stem stitches in light brown and cream embroidery threads to create the reeds. I overlapped the other stitches to make a natural scene.

2 Gradually build up the layers of stitching by adding more reeds. I created the wispy fronds at the top using a mixture of vintage woollen threads. Try different thicknesses of threads to create a richer texture.

3 Use a pencil to darken the end of the reeds. It's a good way of adding another layer of texture to your designs.

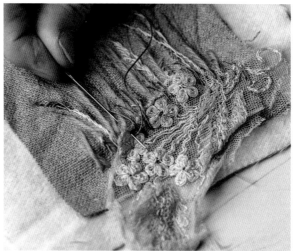

4 Add the piece of lace to the foreground and secure it by working a series of short and long straight stitches over the top end in a random fashion, using a selection of different coloured threads. This gives depth to your design.

5 I added some short lines with a coloured pencil to suggest reeds in shadow at the left edge...

6 ... and some more at the top right. This adds to the texture and sense of depth in your panel.

7 When I was happy the design was finished, I added a small pop of colour using pink silk thread and seed stitch to represent the tiny flash of wildflowers you often see in among the reeds (see page 124 for more on seed stitch).

8 Finally, I used a matching thread and running stitch to stitch around the edge of the panel to secure the edges and stop them from curling up. If you wish, you can fray the edges of the panel a little before stitching. Stitch on any buttons and beads you wish to include at this stage (see the photograph on page 111) . To assemble the bag, see page 116.

*This paper journal shows some of the
written planning and inspiration behind
my dockey bag project.*

*Above are some reeds I drew in a cloth
journal, which I also took inspiration from
for the dockey bag.*

*Left is my finished embroidered panel
for this demonstration. You can see that
my colour palette is quite neutral, as it
represents the patchwork of Fenland fields.
The area is a large producer of crops and
as a result there are fields of different
shades of green and brown surrounding
the ancient wetlands that still remain. You
may, of course, prefer to add more colour
to your own design.*

To create your bag

1 Lay the beige and green linen pieces together with wrong sides facing, tuck under a seam of approximately 1cm (½in) on all edges, and pin the two pieces together.

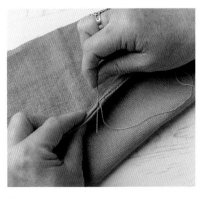

2 Sew them together using an oversew stitch, but leave one short end unstitched – this will be the flap end. The green linen will form the outside and the beige will be the lining.

3 You now have one continuous piece of lined fabric. Next, position the embroidered panel where you want it to go and pin it in place.

4 Attach the finished decorative panel onto the front of your bag with a tacking stitch. You may prefer to create a smaller version of the design so it leaves extra space on your bag, as shown here. I've left the raw edges of the panel as part of the design, but you may wish to neaten yours if you don't enjoy this look.
The flap should overlap the top of the bag by about 10cm (4in).

5 Now sew up the sides of the bag, making your stitching nearly invisible by catching each side of the beige lining and avoiding the green linen.

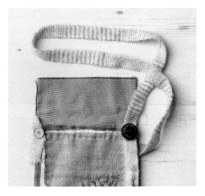

6 Attach a length of woollen blanket to either side of the top using buttons to secure it. Make the strap long enough for the bag to sit comfortably over your shoulder. You may wish to make yours shorter than mine.

Tip

I added an old earring to my strap (see left). I chose it because of its design; it reminds me of my Celtic past and carries a link for me to my Fenland ancestors. Look out for treasures that you can use, as sometimes these little features really personalize your makes.

If you wish, you can add beads and sequins to your panel design as an extra dimension.

As I mentioned before, the workers who traditionally used dockey bags needed quick access to the contents, hence the lack of a closure. I think the raw edges give it a rustic charm.

Tilly's Stitchery

It's always useful to have a reminder of how to work your hand embroidery stitches, so here is a list of all the stitches that I used in the projects for this book, together with some simple step diagrams.

Blanket stitch

So-called because it was traditionally used as an edging for blankets, this is a very useful stitch and one of my favourites.

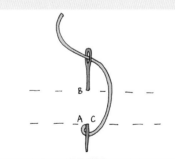

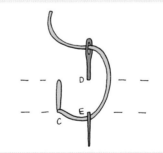

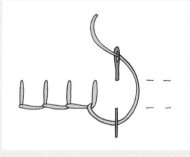

1 Bring the needle up through the fabric at A and pull the thread through. Take it back down at B and up at C, as close as possible to A, keeping the thread under the needle. Pull the thread through to form the first stitch.

2 Insert the needle at D and bring it back out out at E, keeping the thread under the needle while pulling it through. Don't pull the stitches too tightly as this can cause the fabric to pucker.

3 Repeat step 2. To finish, make a small stitch to the right of the final loop, take the thread to the wrong side of the fabric and fasten off.

Buttonhole wheel stitch

This stitch is similar to blanket stitch, except that it is worked in a circle to make a wheel. It can help to mark a circle lightly on your fabric with a pencil first, to achieve a regular shape – although I do like quirky shapes!

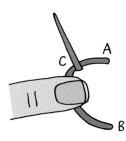
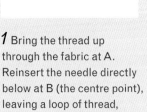

1 Bring the thread up through the fabric at A. Reinsert the needle directly below at B (the centre point), leaving a loop of thread, then bring it back out at C, inside the loop of thread.

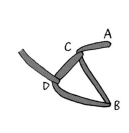

2 Insert the needle into the fabric at B again and bring it out at D, again inside the loop of thread.

3 Repeat the stitch, working your way round the circle shape. Make sure you pull the thread evenly, but not too tightly, to avoid causing the fabric to pucker.

4 The buttonhole wheel is completed.

Chain stitch

Chain stitch is very versatile and doesn't always have to be worked in a straight line. Experiment with it and try wavy lines. It's good as an outlining stitch and as a filling stitch.

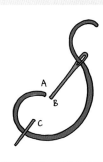

1 Bring the needle up through the fabric at A and pull the thread through. Insert it at B, as close as possible to A, leaving a loop of thread, and bring it up at C. Keep the thread under the needle and pull it through gently to form the first chain. Don't pull the thread too tightly, otherwise you will lose the rounded chain shape.

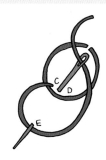

2 Insert the needle at D, as close as possible to C, and bring the needle up through the fabric at E. Keeping the thread under the needle again, pull the thread through gently to make your second chain.

3 Repeat the stitch, making evenly sized chains, until your line is complete. To secure the final stitch, see step 2 for lazy daisy stitch on page 122.

Feather stitch

As my work involves lots of layering of fabrics, I find feather stitch really useful. Not only is it very decorative, but it's also really handy when you want to stitch elements in place or attach appliqué pieces.

1 Bring the thread up through the fabric at B. Reinsert the needle to the right at D, then bring it back out at C, below and between B and D.

2 Next, insert the needle to the left at A, then bring it back out at B.

3 Pull the thread through and reinsert the needle to the left at D and bring it back out at C, but lower down.

4 Continue in this way, working alternately to the right and left, until your line of feather stitch is as long as you want.

Fly stitch

Fly stitch is similar to feather stitch, but it is worked like a Y shape. You can work these singly, as a scattered filling, or in rows or columns, and you can vary the length of the tail.

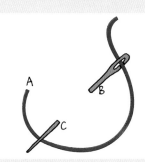 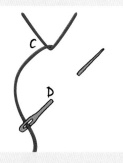 

1 Bring the thread up through the fabric at A. Reinsert the needle to the right at B, then bring it back out at C, below and between A and B.

2 Reinsert the needle below C, at D, and take it out again above and to the right to begin the next stitch directly below the first.

3 The finished stitch forms a Y shape. You can vary the length of the tail, or work this stitch without a tail by reinserting the needle just below point C.

French knots

French knots are great for creating flower centres by making clusters of individual knots, and they also look good scattered around a piece of embroidery. You can make more than two wraps if you want a larger knot.

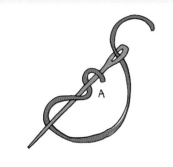

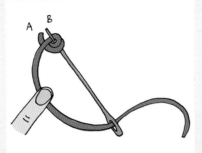

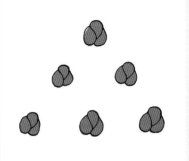

1 Bring the thread through where you want to place the knot, at A. Holding the thread between your thumb and forefinger, wrap it around the needle twice.

2 Hold the thread firmly, close to the needle, and turn the needle back to A. Insert it through the fabric as close to A as possible, at B, and pull the thread through to form a knot.

3 Work as many knots as you wish, then make a small stitch on the wrong side of the fabric and fasten off.

Herringbone stitch

This stitch is made up of crosses that overlap and are not crossed in the middle, but about a quarter of the length of the stitch. If you want to practise, you could draw two parallel lines until you get used to it.

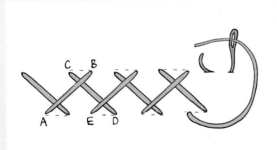

Bring the needle up through the fabric at point A and take it back down at B, above and to the right. Come up again at point C, slightly to the left of B, and take it back down at D. Continue in this way to keep forming stitches.

Star stitch

This is a very simple, but effective, star that is formed by working three straight stitches that cross each other.

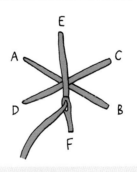

Bring the needle up through the fabric at point A and take it back down at B, diagonally opposite. Bring the needle back up just above it at point C, and down at D. Then bring the needle up at point E and down at F to finish the stitch.

Lazy daisy stitch

With flowers and nature influencing my work most, lazy daisy is a stitch that I use a lot. It's very easy to work and is sometimes called detached chain stitch. You can work the stitches into a flower shape, or singly so they resemble leaves.

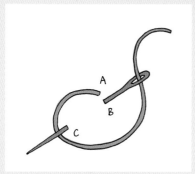 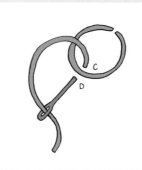 

1 Bring the thread through the fabric at point A, leave a loop of thread, and reinsert the needle at B, as close to A as possible. Bring the needle through at C, so it is inside the loop. Pull the thread through gently to create a petal.

2 Insert the needle at D, taking the thread over the loop, to secure it.

3 Make as many stitches as required, then make a small stitch on the wrong side of your work to secure.

Long and short stitch

This is a series of straight stitches of differing lengths used for filling shapes. If you use diffferent colours, or different shades of the same colour, you can achieve a lovely shaded effect. Adjust the length of the stitches to fit the shape you are filling.

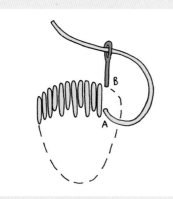  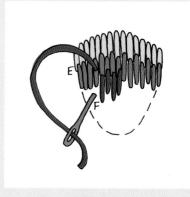

1 Work a row of straight stitches along the top edge of the shape, bringing the needle out at A and in at B. Vary the stitch length, according to the shape to be filled and alternating long and short stitches.

2 Work another row with your next colour, but this time bring the needle out through the stitches at C and in at D. This will give you a nice, flat surface with no gaps. You don't need to split every stitch.

3 Repeat this for the next row, this time coming out at E and in at F. Remember to stagger the stitches to blend the colours. Continue in this way until your shape is filled.

Woven wheel rose stitch

This stitch is great for adding a rose decoration to any embroidery. It is easy to do and it works up quite quickly. However, it does use quite a lot of thread!

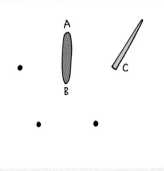

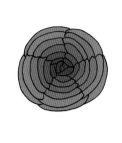

1 Bring the needle up through the fabric at point A and insert it at B, then bring the needle up at point C and down again at B. Continue like this to create five stitches in a star shape.

2 Bring the needle up just next to the middle of the star and weave the thread alternately over and under each arm of the star.

3 Continue in this way to completely cover the arms. Finish the stitch by inserting the needle under the edge and fasten off with a small stitch at the back.

Running stitch

This is the simplest of stitches and is great for making outlines, flower stems and many other things. If you make this stitch a lot larger, it becomes a tacking or basting stitch, used to hold a seam temporarily in place, or attach layers of fabric together.

Bring the needle up through the fabric at point A, insert it at B and bring it up again at C. Continue working along the stitch line, making all your stitches the same length and leaving an equal space between them.

Couching

Couching is worked by laying a thread on the surface of your fabric, and then making small straight stitches over it to hold it in place, usually with a finer thread. It's a fun way to create lines and make interesting colour combinations. I often use couching to hold twigs and sticks in place on my fabric, so that the twig takes the place of the 'laid thread'.

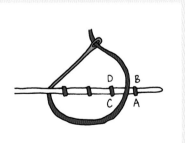

Place the laid thread on your fabric (or you can thread it through from the back if you wish). Thread a needle with the couching thread and bring it up at point A, over the laid thread, and then reinsert it at B. Bring the needle up at point C, then insert it at D. Continue until your laid length of thread is fully couched in position.

Seed stitch

Seed stitch is just a group of small straight stitches made at different angles. They can look really effective as a filling stitch.

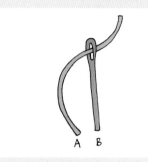

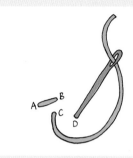

1 Bring the needle up through the fabric at point A and insert it at B to create a tiny straight stitch.

2 Bring the needle back up through at point C and insert it at D to make a second stitch at a different angle.

3 Continue placing your straight stitches randomly until the area you want to cover is filled.

Stem stitch

As the name suggests, stem stitch is perfect to use for the stems of flowers and plants. It creates a beautifully smooth, unbroken line of stitching, and is also great for making outlines.

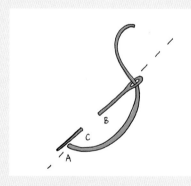

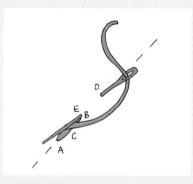

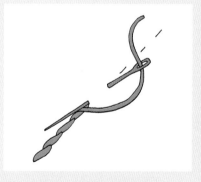

1 Bring the thread up through the fabric at point A and form a loop to the right of your stitching line. Reinsert the needle at point B and bring it out at C, halfway between A and B.

2 Pull the thread through to complete the first stitch. Loop the thread slightly again so it's not in the way, insert the needle at point D and bring it out at E, right next to B.

3 Continue in this way until your line of stitching is complete, always keeping your thread to the right.

Backstitch

Backstitch is quick to work and is great for making outlines or stitching pieces of fabric together. It produces a continuous line of thread without gaps.

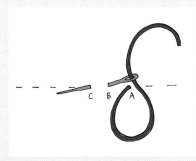
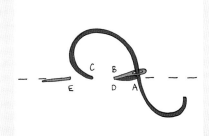

1 Bring your needle up through the fabric at point A, take it back down at B, then up again at C. The gap in between points A and B should be same as the length of the stitch.

2 Pull the thread through, then take the needle back down at point D, then up at E.

3 Continue to work in this way, making sure that your stitches are a consistent length. When you finish, thread your needle through the stitches on the wrong side of the fabric to fasten off.

Satin stitch

This is a filling stitch and you work the stitches very close together in parallel lines to 'colour in' areas of cloth. It can look very effective when used for petals or leaves.

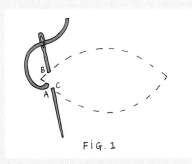
FIG. 1

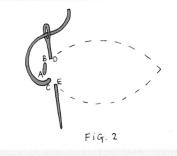
FIG. 2

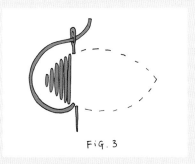
FIG. 3

1 Bring your needle up through the fabric at point A, take it back down at B, then up again at C, just to the right of A.

2 Pull the thread through and then take it back down at point D and up again at E, just to the right of C. The idea is to make a solid shape, so take care to keep your stitches very close together.

3 Repeat the stitch, keeping to the upper and lower edges of the shape you are filling in, until it is complete.

Templates

Jar of Smiles project, page 104

Jar of Smiles

Tales from a Victorian Haberdashery project, page 90
The following doodles were initially used as inspiration
for the needle case project, but you can use them for any
project you like.

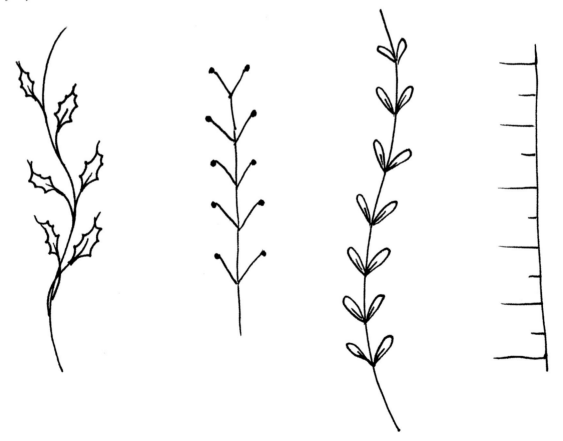

Index